CHICAGO MARCHING

A HISTORY OF PROTEST, AUTHORITY & VIOLENCE

JOSEPH ANTHONY RULLI

THE
History
PRESS

Published by The History Press
Charleston, SC
www.historypress.com

Copyright © 2023 by Joseph Anthony Rulli
All rights reserved

First published 2023

Manufactured in the United States

ISBN 9781467151436

Library of Congress Control Number: 2022948305

*First they came for the socialists, and
I did not speak out—
Because I was not a socialist.*

*Then they came for the trade unionists, and
I did not speak out—
Because I was not a trade unionist.*

*Then they came for the Jews, and
I did not speak out—
Because I was not a Jew.*

*Then they came for me—and
there was no one left to speak for me.*

—Reverend Martin Niemöller, 1946

Illusion is the most tenacious weed in the collective consciousness; history teaches, but it has no students: working class tears could not be wiped away by machine gun blasts.

—*Antonio Gramsci,* Ordine Nuovo (The New Order)*, 1921*

DEDICATION

This book is dedicated to all who have held or are holding positions on the lower rungs of the social ladder. Let this work be for the unemployed and homeless, the artists in the labor force and creating in their "off" time, for workers in the service industries, farm and office workers, public transportation staffs, teachers, aides and school staffs, customer service employees, wait staffers, cooks, housekeepers, cashiers, healthcare professionals, receptionists and clerks—those who know what it means to "bite your tongue" because we need the job. This book is for all whose healthcare is tied to these jobs, to those who should be enjoying retirement but keep working because of the inadequate insurance coverage without employment.

This is dedicated to all those who have come before us, having provided what we possess now—those who sacrificed and bled in their push from the bottom up yesterday to attain the blessings we enjoy today and hopefully more may enjoy tomorrow; to all those who have immigrated from one place to another, or who still struggle with this in a world of too many walls and too few bridges; to all those whose movement from home to elsewhere was forced and in chains. Let this book lift up all who consider everyone as part of the grand *us*.

CONTENTS

LIST OF PHOTOGRAPHS

ACKNOWLEDGEMENTS

This book being my third work of nonfiction with The History Press/Arcadia Publishing and my fourth book overall, it is clear that I have had a lot of support in my life. As always, my first shout-outs go to my family: I have been granted a support system now for over half a century, and even though our parents, Felix Salvatore Rulli and Catherine Marie (Palmero) Rulli, have gone on to another home, their spirits still flow in Cathy alongside Bill Kazmierczak, Michael and Sarah Kazmierczak, Samantha Kazmierczak and Terri Rulli. We also have been blessed with an extended family that could count as a small army! But not being of a warmongering spirit, the extended families on the Rulli and Palmero sides and all connected branches of the family in this country, the mountains of Campania and Calabria and the southern Italian and Sicilian coasts have given me love and history and a pride that exceeds any possible honors on a battlefield.

My love of history and writing was fostered at home as well as in school. I am always grateful for my friends and teachers at St. John the Baptist School and St. Joseph High School as well as the History Department at the University of Notre Dame and the monks and other professors at St. Meinrad School of Theology. The Alexis Coquillard Public School Library remained open during the summers of my childhood, and I appreciate the growth that happened in me because of the staff there.

To the staff and supporters of the Chicago History Museum, especially the Abakanowicz Research Center and the Rights and Reproduction Department as they reopened in the midst of ongoing pandemic concerns and protocols. To Ellen Keith, Lesley Martin, Colleen Layton, Michael Featherstone and Brigid Crawley. To the staff at the Newberry Library, the archivists and staffs of the University of Illinois–Chicago Library, the University of Chicago, Loyola University's Women and Leadership Archives, the Chicago Urban League, the Chicago Public Library and photographers Antonio Perez and Jyoti Srivastava. The dedication shown by you all in the preservation of the historical record is inspiring.

To the city of Chicago: Even though the bureaucratic side receives an abundance of criticism from me, I am always grateful for the organization and attempts at making life here better. My gratitude, as always, extends to the Chicago Transit Authority and Metra Lines for my relative ease of travel throughout the city and suburbs—it may not always be as smooth as it could be, but it is workable, and I appreciate the attempts at improving it. Again, to the Chicago Police Department in their ongoing efforts in public safety alongside the vigilance over their own accountability in cooperation with civilian boards.

To my wiz team of people who helped make this third history book better. I appreciate my photographer, Nathanael Filbert, and his staff, past and present, for the work they've done for me; to MacDaniel Sullivan, my web designer; to my financial guide, Mark Willis. To Steve Bellinger, my "partner in grime," I will always treasure our friendship as we continue digging into history in fiction and nonfiction; and to Donna Smith-Bellinger, my "partner with the vine" and a guiding voice of encouragement and challenge to "sell, don't tell!"

To the staff of The History Press and Arcadia Publishing for their belief and excitement in this, our third project together, especially to Ben Gibson, my commissioning editor and ready ear and voice to help make this a better book as he has done with the previous two works, and to Abigail Fleming, senior copyeditor. To my publisher of my first novel, the satire *Bread & Circuses*, Andy Holsteen of Shy City House, for his keen literary sense, cooperation with recording it in audiobook form and his commitment to social justice in SCH's donation of 5 percent of all sales to the author's charity of choice (Storycatchers Theatre)—and especially for his and Morgan Gray's friendship.

As always, now past my fifteenth year at Trader Joe's on Clybourn Avenue, my co-workers and managers at the store have been an amazing presence in my life. And going through over two years of pandemic protocols, supply chain issues and general retail craziness the load has been made much easier with great people to share the burdens and most especially the laughs. And also, thanks to the Trader Joe's Company that has employed me this long, helping me earn a living, allowing me the luxury of my writing time. To my muse, Tyler Jason Fortaleza Claytor, "Hyacinthus in Greek times," for trust and friendship, for encouragement, the reality checks and for being a ready ear to listen to this work as it developed.

To my comrades in the socialist, anarchist and communist camps: though it's difficult "to play nice" with each other all the time, your passionate and peaceful presence in the city still proves to me that liberty has a strong voice, and it's more powerful than the one barked from the mainstream media and politicians. To those who march for anyone's rights, even when some of those rights seem to be in direct opposition to each other: Everyone's peaceful march is a powerful voice against the creeping brutality of megalomania and totalitarianism we see growing. To my comrade, friend, inspiration for the audiobooks I have created and fellow writer Robert Kingett, a courageous spokesman, who, being blind, can see what others cannot.

As with my previous two books, I reserve final appreciation for all laborers of the past and in all places. Their sacrifices, their words and deeds, sometimes whispered and oftentimes shouted from the mountaintops, have been rallying cries of life in a world too often concerned with the drudgery of work for its own sake. Their blood, sweat and tears have reaped a harvest of a more just society than was known 150 years ago. And though we've not come as far as some had hoped, we have come further than many have dreamed because of them.

Liberty, equality, fraternity to all!

DREAMS DEFERRED, DOWNSIZED, DESTROYED?

Sincerely and earnestly hoping that this little book may do something toward throwing light on the American slave system, and hastening the glad day of deliverance to the millions of my brethren in bonds—faithfully relying upon the power of truth, love, and justice, for success in my humble efforts—and solemnly pledging myself anew to the sacred cause.
—*Frederick Douglass,* Narrative of the Life of Frederick Douglass, *April 28, 1845*

As quite possibly the greatest speaker of the nineteenth century, with the keenest insight into the reality of slavery up to his own day, a twenty-year-old Fredrick Douglass saw his dream of freedom realized on September 3, 1838, as he reached New York. By the time of his death in 1895, he had risen to the level first of "Father of the Abolition Movement" and later as the voice of equality, offering wisdom he would pass on to African American newspapers like the *Chicago Defender* as well as the burgeoning civil rights movements of the next century.

By the middle of the twentieth century, Douglass's legacy had continued. Langston Hughes (1901–1967) and Martin Luther King Jr. (1929–1968) wrote and spoke of dreams: one was a warning of what *might be* if the dreams were put off, while the other was a proclamation of what *could be* if they were embraced. In the over half a century since Hughes's and King's deaths, American society has bounded, bounced and bumbled its way between the two. Sometimes the journey was like a climber heading to the mountaintop, other times like a pinball out of the chute, clanging with a lot of noise and no direction except a path seemingly, and depressingly, destined to lead to the swamp muck of history repeating itself.

Chicago Marching: A History of Protest, Authority and Violence is a study of the people's struggles with their dreams in the "Second City," the "Windy City," beginning before the metropolis received these names and up to our own day. This book is an analysis of the dreams of its diverse people: How were these dreams expressed? What happens to the dreams when they butt up against a civil authority interpreting some dreams with preconceived ideas of them and of the dreamers themselves? And what has happened in Chicago over the nearly two centuries when, as Hughes observed, the dreams were deferred?

One must first ask, "What dreams are we talking about?" Fair enough. The dreams of Chicagoans since the incorporation of the city on March 4, 1837, were those of the founders of every city or settlement since pre-history—security, a livelihood to provide for themselves and loved ones, a sense of independence, of self-sufficiency with no encroachment from hostile groups be they in the cave next door or in city council chambers downtown. Though the challenges of people have varied over the millennia, from saber-toothed tigers to intercontinental ballistic missiles, the root desire is to live as peacefully and securely as possible. In spite of overlords, farmers, invaders, Natives, industrialists and workers, people generally want to reap the benefits of organized society equitably.

In the United States, the ultimate attempt to forge a workable set of laws governing the nation has been the Constitution. While not perfect, it is the ability of citizens to amend the original document that has been its real strength. Knowing this fact as being part of the intent of the framers of the government at the end of the eighteenth century, and being well aware of their biases and flaws, we should have a realistic attitude concerning the permanence or temporality of any part of its contents. Many of the founders of this democratic republic were slaveholders, shipbuilders and sailors who fueled the slave trade or were secondhand beneficiaries of the slave system. The framers consciously excluded women from full participation in the new government, and they denied the full humanity of those with darker skin color brought to the hemisphere.

With the flaws of the "scientists" of the Great Experiment being unquestioned reality, one must ask why we consider them and the Constitution they wrote to be infallible. That is to say, they were flawed human beings and wrote a flawed document—it needed ten immediate amendments (the Bill of Rights) before it would be acceptable to all of the original thirteen states. There has always been a tendency to consider the document perfectly worded, understandable and applicable to all situations. Most constitutional conflicts are argued on the basis of a literal interpretation or one based on the sense of the articles held within it. There are ways of knowing "what the framers intended" based on other contemporary documents like the *Federalist Papers*, but also it is important to courageously debate the essentials of what we do today with issues the framers had no idea were to develop.

One can accept the Second Amendment and still discuss its limitations in the wake of mass murders with assault rifles and the unbridled gun trade throughout American streets—something that hadn't played out at all to the founders in the 1780s. One can add to this the apparent phallic attachment of males to their guns in the twentieth and twenty-first centuries. In addition, while an individual's privacy is not overtly stated in the Fourth Amendment's protection against unreasonable and unwarranted searches and seizures, it is implied in its first sentence regarding the right of an individual "in their persons, houses, papers, and effects." The issues of recent history and our own time regarding abortion rights, same-sex marriage and contraception can be debated in relation to the implied constitutional protections of the Fourth Amendment without any besmirching of the lily-white aura of the document or its authors.

Any historical study needs to be as balanced as possible without falling into a relativistic view of the past that condemns nothing and excuses everything. Careful word choices are essential: one person's legacy of slavery can be seen as another's regrettable economic expansion; one industrialist pulling himself up by his bootstraps is another's vision of the crushing foot on the neck of the worker; one's riot is another's voice unmuffled; one's attempt to preserve the peace is another's autocratic repression; a group of people can be seen as either a ruthless invader or a colonist. Without sanitizing the historical record, the student of history must uncover as much of the truth as possible, the "What actually happened?" of the past. The accepted cultural narrative, the "This is the way I was taught" philosophy, is not the whole story. And if we are to come to any semblance of peaceful coexistence within society, we had better begin to look at things more as light is refracted into a rainbow rather than like black-and-white letters in newsprint or as the default font color on computer screens.

This work seeks to be a balanced study of the events that have unfolded when the needs and desires of various groups have clashed in Chicago. Not simply a rehash of violent protests from 1855 to the present, *Chicago Marching* looks at the root causes of what oftentimes begin as peaceful airings of grievances or impassioned expressions of rights but devolve into violence; it's also a comparative study of how civil authority through the years has acted/reacted to the challenges, threats and opportunities of coming face to face (metaphorically and sometimes literally) with the people supposedly being served.

The global pandemic of the early 2020s provided us with many learning opportunities due to remote and virtual everything. One of them, for those who notice things of this nature, could be seen in the majority of interviews done with politicians via the internet: the ubiquitous bookcase-in-the-background was readily available to showcase that particular person's choice of literature, and it was inevitably, with very few exceptions, full of nonfiction. Now, let it be understood (especially in a book of nonfiction!) that this genre is noble and essential. However, it is telling of a certain defect of creativity when one upholds the exclusivity of this one type of writing so that one may appear scholarly. Apparently, the only time politicians are seen possessing fiction is in their campaign advertising during election season!

Elected officials are comfortable with absolutes in their speeches but fumble into the gray of the "iffy" in press conferences. The flaw of the public is in accepting this as legitimate leadership: we appreciate facts that are simple, clear, quantifiable, categorical, whether they're true or not. We're comfortable with seeing things as absolute and in the realm of the "-ism." Something is this or that, capitalism or socialism, Black or white, gay or "straight," male or female. We settle into camps of agreement about economics, race, orientation, gender. It's either racism or it's not; it's homophobia or not; it's sexism or it isn't.

In the summer of 2020, people in this country experienced a wave of iconoclasm, of statue busting, that swept into many cities. In this writer's opinion, it was a fascinating phenomenon to witness as the vandalism of monuments and numerous municipal actions and reactions from east to west highlighted a powerful historical reality: statues and monuments are expressions of the values of a people at particular periods of time, and sometimes those things that have been upheld change. The amphitheater in Rome is still known as the Colosseum even after the *colossal* statue of Nero that had originally stood in front of it was torn down after his death.

And to see a similar type of attitudinal change in its early expressions in 2020 was a definite historical moment. The most dramatic and moving event in this regard quite possibly was the bipartisan decision in the Mississippi legislature, with the support of the governor, to eliminate the Stars and Bars, the infamous design of the Confederate battle flag, from the state flag. It was a great symbolic gesture in the ongoing struggle for a reckoning of slavery that this nation must further advance. Whether one is discussing the Confederate flag or statues of Confederate generals, Christopher Columbus or William Jefferson Clinton, we as a people have to confront past values that have been held, and that might need to be changed in this pluralistic society we have created.

While most histories have been written from a largely Euro–North American perspective of military action and territorial conquest of white males, new perspectives have emerged and continue to develop that ease the burden of constructing studies of the past from a multifaceted angle. One interesting nugget uncovered, though certainly not a solitary discovery, is the absence in collected material of violent clashes between authority holders and women in Chicago's past. Notwithstanding the arrests and beatings that women have received as they protested in the city, and certainly not ignoring the firebrand speechmaking of leading women like socialist pioneer Lucy Parsons, alongside the in-your-face words, actions and writings of Ida B. Wells-Barnett, Jane Addams and Josephine Conger-Kaneko, the actions of women in Chicago have been powerful in their own right, without resorting as readily to violence as their male comrades and city authorities.

Women's suffrage parade, May 2, 1914, the first year that Illinois women were allowed to vote in statewide and national elections. *Courtesy of the Chicago History* Museum (DN-0062519).

Is it in the way people are wired? Are some more likely to hold onto power or grasp for power as a type of testosterone territorialism, the proverbial "pissing contest" or size comparison? Or is it something simpler? Is it just the historical reality that in most places and through most times males have happened to be in control and have clung to that power out of a human impulse that is shared regardless of gender, as can also be seen in the few matriarchal societies in the past of which we are aware? This subject necessitates a study in itself and is mentioned here as a pointer to others for further work into the Chicago protest experiences.

History is inclusive in that all people of all times and places are a part of it. The truth of the matter is that people, and their beliefs, can be complex and are on a spectrum. All people possess reasons for holding particular positions, and no matter what those reasons are, the path to societal harmony lies in understanding the reasons as well as the people themselves who hold the positions. It's the hope that this work will assist along this path. The intention here is not to detail the events of each civic disturbance or uprising in Chicago's history but to use each major event as a doctor might study cases. It's the hope here that through an overview of events of causal similarities and differences, along with the repercussions of each instance, one can come to conclusions that may help find creative solutions to contemporary social challenges.

I

THE OLD SETTLERS CLUB

But the British ruling class obviously could not admit to themselves that their
usefulness was at an end. Had they done that they would have had to abdicate.
For it was not possible for them to turn themselves into mere bandits, like the
American millionaires, consciously clinging to unjust privileges and beating down
opposition by bribery and tear-gas bombs.
—*George Orwell,* The Lion and the Unicorn, *1940*

ALL ANIMALS ARE EQUAL, BUT SOME ANIMALS ARE MORE EQUAL THAN OTHERS

What was written by the English author George Orwell as German bombs fell around him during the London Blitz rang true a century before he set it down on paper. Those in power, historically, seem to ignore the fact that their legitimacy to that potency is being questioned. They focus their attention on clinging to that power like the grip of a person in the throes of imminent death. Chicago was no different. From the beginning, it drew people from across the country to establish their brand of civilization decades after the Native peoples had been cleared away.

In 1836, one year before the city of Chicago was incorporated and two decades before the Illinois legislature passed the most restrictive race-based legislation (Black Laws) of any northern state, soon-to-be-mayor William

Butler Ogden conceived a plan to build the region's first railroad. Even though the railway wouldn't become reality until the next decade, Ogden was able to harness the economic energies of the newborn American elite in the westernmost states along with powerful connections in Washington, D.C., to secure federal funding to build the Illinois and Michigan Canal as the precursor to the railroad.

One downtown hotel, the Tremont House at the intersection of Lake and Dearborn Streets, saw the clear delineation of those who belonged in the city and those who were allowed to be here by the grace of those who belonged. In its third incarnation, the swanky hotel boasted in 1851 that $30,000 ($1 million in 2021 purchasing power) had been spent just on furnishings, including the hotel bar, which would play host to exclusivity with the Old Settlers Club. Membership to this organization was extended to the acknowledged founding families of Chicago—the Ogdens, the Wentworths, the Gurnees and the Kinzies, descendants of War of 1812 veteran and errantly reputed first non-Native resident of Chicago John Kinzie. Jean Baptiste Point du Sable of the island of Ay-ti (formerly known as Saint Domingue and present-day Haiti) would be granted the rightful title

Bust of Chicago's first non-Native resident, Jean Baptiste Point du Sable, near the convergence of the Chicago River and Lake Michigan, where he and his wife, Kitihawa (Catherine), lived. *Courtesy of the author.*

a century and a half later but would not have been granted admission to the club of old settlers (nor would his wife, Kitihawa of the Potawatomi tribe) because of his skin color had he stuck around to have attempted admittance.

In less than a decade, it became clear what would speak loudest in the growing metropolis—money, land or friendly politicians in local, state and national government, along with a print mouthpiece in any of Chicago's many newspapers.

The interconnectedness of the ruling class with the burgeoning industrialists must be understood in order to grasp the significance of every piece of legislation passed, appropriation of federal or state funding granted or restrictions lifted that aided business owners or stockholders, to the exclusion of any others. Nature may grant talent and drive unequally, to paraphrase Jean-Jacques Rousseau, but it is human beings gathered into a society that have the power to grant or deny equality of *opportunity* to all. That's where the stories of human progress and regression expose the blatant inequity between the haves and have-nots of societies in every place, through every age.

Cyrus and Leander McCormick were two of the earliest easterners who migrated to Chicago. By 1847, they had established themselves as the premier manufacturer of harvesting equipment in the country (with the help of free advertising in newspapers like the *Weekly Chicago Democrat*, owned by future mayor and congressman John Wentworth). The company received a boost after a series of letters to the editor in the aforementioned paper; it printed a total of six testimonials about the new McCormick reaper machines, one of them signed by Cyrus Hall McCormick himself.

With federal land grants beginning to be bestowed with regal grace, from the lands of the nations who had occupied the continent before the Europeans, the powerbrokers in Washington, D.C., confirmed the prejudices of past generations (and of generations yet to come) by favoring the growing conglomerates of the newborn railway system and those men wealthy enough to profit from them. Several citizens like Wentworth took the opportunity to become stock owners in the Illinois Central line, have influence in job distribution and take control of the direction of lucrative lakefront improvements.

Like an epic struggle between two mythological beasts, Wentworth and Senator Stephen A. Douglas bought property from the railroad for lakefront homes and went head to head with city officials; Mayor Walter Gurnee, another homeowner on the lake, vetoed the results of a referendum of the city's white adult male property owners, which Wentworth and Douglas supported, who wanted to grant right-of-way passage up the lakeshore to the railways. An agreement was eventually reached that would allow train traffic through the city's shoreline for generations. By 1856, ten rail lines connected in Chicago, with thirty-eight freight and fifty-eight passenger trains leaving the city every day. By the beginning of the Civil War, most railroads in the country met in the city. None of these initiatives were bad in themselves; the detrimental effect was in the exclusion of the majority of the population in decision-making, which seemed to accompany any discussion or decision that would affect the entire city.

With a population of under 30,000, the issue of labor became an essential question to answer regarding canal and railroad construction. At that same time, in 1848, with political tensions in Europe strained by a series of revolutions in France as well as in pre-unified Germany and Italy, and

Photographs by Hesler.

No. 12. Hon. JOHN WENTWORTH, Mayor.

No. 1. Alderman	KENDALL.	10. Alderman	KENNEDY.
2. "	SCHMIDT.	11. "	D'WOLF.
3. "	HARRIS.	13. "	SITTS.
4. "	GREENEBAUM.	14. "	DIVERSEY.
5. "	LA RUE.	15. "	GREEN.
6. "	CONLEY.	16. "	BROSS.
7. "	MYERS.	17. "	DUNLAP.
8. "	CARTER.	18. "	WAHL.
9. "	KREISMAN,	19. "	LONG.
	(City Clerk.)	20. "	JOY.

Biographical notices will be given in our next No.

Mayor John Wentworth and Chicago's aldermen, 1857. *Courtesy of the Chicago History Museum (i82674_pm).*

with a massive famine in Ireland reaching unimaginable proportions, this new city built on an onion-smelling swamp (*checagou*, as called by those who were living there when Columbus was lost at sea) became the answer to the political and economic sufferings of the new group of immigrants. Within a decade and a half, these newcomers would raise Chicago's population to well over 100,000. Laborers from China and Japan would arrive later and face similar experiences as the railroads reached to the Pacific Ocean.

The opportunities brought by these new modes of transportation also had accompanying tensions. By way of reaction, a new concept of "Americanism" sprouted as this new and poorer group from Europe immigrated to the East Coast and the Great Lakes region. White settlers who had first moved into the region primarily from New England brought with them the proverbial Protestant work ethic, a puritanical sense of morality, alongside the we/they dichotomy that has plagued this country for over four centuries, predating independence.

Even though the early days of the city were fraught with gunslinging, prostitution and drunkenness of the Wild West type, those who would rise to leadership positions by the time of that first wave of immigration set about to define (and limit) what inclusion meant. Those in power feared political instability from the new philosophy set out by Karl Marx and Friedrich Engels that accompanied the Germans, and they held the Irish in disdain for their very non-Anglo ways. But this was not unique to the Chicago experience, nor was it limited to European immigration.

The North's Black Curtain

While the fear of the outsider, or xenophobia, was newly placed on this group of immigrants to the region and it would continue to rise up periodically through the nineteenth, twentieth and twenty-first centuries, the American dread of the *other* is double rooted: in the first place, the fear (or possibly guilt) is a visceral response to the Native peoples who had been dwelling on the continent for thousands of years prior to Europeans bumping into the land mass and pushing westward. Secondly, it reaches into our cultural bowels because of the unbridled slave trade in which both northerners and southerners were complicit for 250 years. Since 1619, when the first Africans were forced onto ships and brought to North and South America, the twisted mentality that promoted the idea of human beings enslaving other human beings saw the growing specter of open revolt, as well as the fear of racial equality that began in the decades after the Civil War. Thomas Jefferson stated this double fear with reference to slavery in his 1781 *Notes on the State of Virginia*:

> *Indeed, I tremble for my country when I reflect that God is just: that his justice cannot sleep for ever: that considering numbers, nature and natural means only, a revolution of the wheel of fortune, an exchange of situation, is among possible events: that it may become probable by supernatural interference! The Almighty has no attribute which can take side with us in such a contest.*

Those who saw great potential in the newborn City on the Lake were visionaries who became the spokesmen for Chicago's growth. Early boosters like Ogden, Wentworth and future mayor Levi Boone, among many others, viewed themselves as builders, organizers and molders of not only the structures of the physical city but also the structures of society; it was clear to them that they were most capable to achieve this. They were the movers, the doers and the conductors who would tell others what they needed to do (and not do) if they wished to be part of the community.

And this new order would confirm the values of the old guard: women would have limited roles, in spite of their voices trumpeting louder than ever almost immediately after the city's incorporation through the growing suffrage, abolition and Prohibition movements; free Black people living in Illinois were hardly free and would be severely restricted because of their skin color, the state having codified intolerance in its first constitution in 1818 through the notorious Black Laws; and immigrants from anywhere but northern Europe would be relegated to relentless labor, feeding the industrial beast that had just begun to belch its oppression through steam, smoke and steel. Individuals in these poorer groups relied on themselves, for better and worse, sometimes pitting themselves against other outsiders, to create a livelihood for their families in this new land of backroom promises and often found that while they lived on the land, the promise for them would be elusive—or more to the point, it would be kept out of their reach.

Since the "best people," the Optimates, as the ancient Romans called the ruling class, knew what was best for the city, their attitudes toward the outsiders reflected a paternalism in keeping with an imperial mindset. As mayors, both Ogden and Boone accepted the prevailing opinions of an American society that had just begun to venture across the Appalachian Mountains a couple of generations earlier: hard work was the way to

The two-thousand-year-old Roman pillar standing near Soldier Field, the gift of Italy's Benito Mussolini to the people of Chicago to commemorate Italo Balbo's 1934 transatlantic flight—the Fascist emblems were later removed. *Courtesy of the author.*

success, cutting a path through godless wilderness, with the Anglo–Northern European branch of Christianity igniting the fire that would give the frontier its purity.

Anything outside this world view was a threat: The Native peoples, in the view of the rulers, needed to be subdued as well as converted from their ungodly ways; the enslaved and free Black populations were to be kept in bondage, either through physical chains or legislation; and the "poor and vicious foreigners living in shanties and rookeries," in the words of Mayor Ogden, were fit only for working in the industries of the growing cities.

It's a sign of the impoverished thought of rulers when conditions of fellow human beings are allowed to become desperate enough that fear of revolt remains in the forefront of the ruler's mind. Rather than addressing the wrongs that the powerful have committed against the weak and thereby decreasing the chances of revolt, the typical response of the controllers has been to clamp down on rebellion with vigorous force. When Thomas Jefferson wrote the Declaration of Independence, one of the accusations against King George III was that "he has excited domestic insurrections amongst us and has endeavored to bring on…the merciless Indian Savages." The future third president couldn't see the tragedy of his self-righteousness concerning not only the Native tribes he mentions but also the millions of enslaved people whom the British had been coaxing with freedom in exchange for their loyalty to the Crown in the revolt of the white gentry in the thirteen colonies.

Nikole Hannah-Jones, in her piece titled "Justice," toward the end of the series of essays and poems in *The 1619 Project*, calls the Jeffersonian attitude "intentional forgetting" (alive and well in the twenty-first century), and it must be confronted if the legacies of slavery and the dispossession of Native lands from the original settlers are to be fully confronted and exorcized from this society. She states:

> *The racism we are fighting today was originally conjured to justify working unfree Black people, often until death, to generate extravagant riches for European colonial powers, the white planter class, and all ancillary white people, from Midwestern farmers to bankers to sailors to textile workers, who earned their living and built their wealth from that free Black labor and the products their labor produced. The prosperity of this country is inextricably linked with the forced labor of the ancestors of more than 30 million Black Americans, just as it is linked to the stolen land of the country's Indigenous people. Though our high school text books seldom*

make this plain, slavery and the hundred-year period of racial apartheid and racial terrorism known as Jim Crow were, above all else, systems of economic exploitation.

What the textbooks need, what the school systems are required to do, what each citizen would be wise to accept is a bold grip on the retelling of the history of this country at the expense of the limp, whitewashed fiction that has passed for American history in the collective memory through generations of an accepted mythological curricula. Antonio Gramsci, one of the founders of the Italian Communist Party in 1921 and early opponent of and martyr to Benito Mussolini's totalitarianism, developed a philosophy called *hegemony* as it applies to culture and history. He promoted a systemic recalibration of cultural institutions, the main tool, according to the philosophy, of capitalist control of society. He held that the proletariat, the working class, needed to recast the cultural narrative in addition to ousting the traditional institutions of the church/state binary. The main avenue to this revolution would be through education, especially in the retelling of the story of a people's history through the eyes of the working class rather than through political machinations, military conquests and imperialist justifications through the perspective of an upper-class male bloodline of stories.

Gramsci's hegemony is at the root of what is called critical race theory. This theory seeks to upend how American history has been communicated so that it stands on solid feet and not on its head as it presently does. Contrary to the visceral reaction of those who misunderstand the concept and hear only "blaming white people," critical race theory allows people to understand just how significant a role race has played in the formation of this country and the modern world.

Critical race theory highlights two historical realities: first, it is indisputable that the race-based slave trade allowed imperial European/Asian powers and the newly independent United States three centuries of wealth that has built most of the nations of the Northern Hemisphere into the haves and a majority of the peoples of the Southern Hemisphere into the have nots. The developed world or "first and second worlds" exist in large part because of the existence of the developing world, or "third world," for the past five hundred years.

And second, the theory is grounded in the other ugly reality that since the sixteenth century and, in the United States, through the century after the Civil War, skin color has been the litmus test for economic, political and educational opportunity. The American experience of racial inequity is another unarguable truth: race-based lynchings; the bombings of homes, businesses and churches; the color line of segregation in neighborhoods, beaches, schools, jobs and labor unions; the inequity of both voting opportunities and the attainment of political office; and the added horror of the apparent shoot-to-kill orders aimed predominantly against young Black and Brown men and boys that seem to have been promulgated nationwide has left a bloodstained path of death, suspicion and violence that we are still witnessing well into the first quarter of the twenty-first century.

With the exception of the Native peoples, no other group has been expelled from acquired lands as the freed Black population was during the Andrew Johnson presidency; no group has had to face death by hanging because they dared to look at a white man or (God forbid) a white woman, or open a business, or defied prejudice to stand in line to vote as the freed

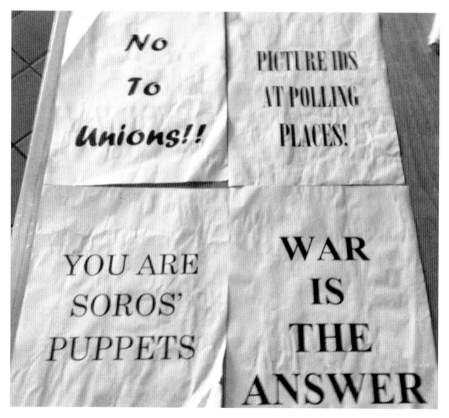

Various handbills thrown down at marchers from the upper floors of the Chicago Board of Trade building, May Day 2014. *Courtesy of the author.*

Black population did after federal troops were pulled out of the defeated Confederacy. This exclusion was the result of the Republican and Democratic Parties colluding against freed citizens after the election of 1876. And no other group has needed armed guards, state militias or federal troops to escort them to school as African American children and young adults did in the 1950s and 1960s. No other group has needed to have three constitutional amendments and two congressional civil rights or voting rights acts passed to protect basic freedoms that have been enjoyed by other Americans from the nation's founding.

The fear of losing power, losing a seat at the table, of "them" taking over from "us," is key to understanding the willful ignorance to reject the simple historical facts required for the true reckoning specifically of slavery's legacy and generally in how the powerful have kept control in the United States. There is enough room at the table for everyone, but each one gets only one seat! For too long, this country has seen itself as a ship: there is first class, and there is steerage. It's been all too clear who belongs in which section of the liner.

Perhaps subconsciously, perhaps not so much so, the romanticizing of the one narrative of American history that has been promulgated is similar to a dysfunctional family's denial of its own abusive past in the attempt to move past the pain. If one member of the family seeks to address a painful experience or a series of traumas, the typical reaction can be a visceral onslaught of most of the family against the one, the identified patient, as they are called in family systems counseling. But bringing the issues fully to the surface is the only healthy way to expunge the tragedies and pain of the past. A family cannot move forward in health without such a confrontation, and a nation cannot find real societal reconciliation without a similar reckoning.

Huddled Masses and Wretched Refuse before the Statue of Liberty

While less horrific than slavery and its aftermath but intolerable nonetheless, the immigrant experience of the last century and a half has exposed similar ethnic-based prejudiced attitudes of a ruling elite against outsiders and newcomers. These groups chose to cross over an ocean for the same reasons that the ancestors of those who held power in Chicago crossed. In search of a better life through economic opportunity as well as political and religious

Chicago mayors, 1837–1885. *Courtesy of the Chicago History Museum (i029213_pm).*

freedom, large numbers of eastern and southern Europeans followed the Irish to the growing city. Yet they were met with similar resistance.

Mayor Levi Boone, in his 1855 inaugural address, tried to play the politician in his speech but simply exposed the prevailing prejudices of the day by his word choices: "I have only to discover the broad seal of humanity… my brother…his friend." And in the same speech, he reveals typical WASP (White Anglo-Saxon Protestant) bigotry: "[We] cannot be blind to the existence in our midst of a powerful politico-religious organization…[the] spiritual supremacy of a foreign despot" (read, "the Roman Catholic pope"). However, in spite of itself, the leadership in the city would begin a gradual practice of acceptance and absorption of a few outsiders into the ruling elite: within a generation, more Irish and German Catholics would join the growing Chicago Police Department as well as be given control of the security of the city after disaster, namely the Irish Catholic general Philip Sheridan in the weeks after the 1871 fire.

The American experience mirrors, slightly, that of Ancient Rome with regard to citizenship: almost two thousand years before the Constitution was written, Roman elite struggled with the question of granting full benefit of imperial citizenship. In the generation before Gaius Julius Caesar reached for sole power, the peoples of the Italian peninsula were granted full citizenship. Mike Duncan observed in *The Storm Before the Storm: The Beginning of the End of the Roman Republic*, that "the voice of the Roman citizen was not lost, it simply changed pitch with the addition of new voices." Today, with nationalism on the rise again, as we slide further away from a positive definition of globalism, citizenship has become one of many fuses that threatens to ignite the explosives lying underneath society. And once again, as it did shortly after Chicago's founding, a narrow definition of "American" has become positive, while "foreign" is used almost exclusively in the pejorative sense.

The root of the attitudes toward Native Americans, enslaved and free Black Americans as well as southern/eastern Europeans, Asian immigrants and others lies in the fear these groups engender by being different—either in skin tone, dress, worldviews, lifestyles, gender identification, worship or politics. Stereotypes often held by the old guard are trotted out to solidify preconceived notions of the newcomer and the different. Compartments are created when a person's view is confirmed: someone is seen drinking excessively, or is loud, or commits a crime, or is lazy, and not to mention those who are flamboyant, or dress like the opposite sex, and society's gavel slams on its bench in judgment. Laws have been written to deal with this tide of undesirability and exclude the undesirables.

John J. Flinn, nineteenth-century historian of the Chicago Police, was no friend to the immigrant-filled labor ranks, but he gave indictment against the exclusivity of the American Party (the Know-Nothings) in those early years of Chicago's history. In his 1887 *History of the Chicago Police*, he said:

> [An] *illustration of the length to which race prejudice was permitted to extend can be found then in the fact that every applicant for employment under the city administration* [by 1855] *was compelled to prove that he had been born on American soil.*

Codification of prejudices has been the go-to tactic of power-wielders in the United States, the state of Illinois and the city of Chicago from the beginning. The notorious Three-Fifths Clause of the U.S. Constitution remained intact from 1788 until the passage of the Thirteenth Amendment in 1865, which dismantled the structure of chattel slavery and the dehumanization of the enslaved. The original clause declared every slave was to be counted as three-fifths of a person for the electoral benefit of southern states. That concession, so instrumental for the newly independent country, would wound the American body politic to a near-mortal level through bloody civil war; it would leave the wound infected well into the twentieth century through apartheid legislation of the Jim Crow laws of both southern and northern states, even as it still seeps pus in our own day.

Taking its cue from the federal government, Illinois ratified its constitution in 1818, becoming the twenty-first state, and eventually passed some of the strictest race-based laws of any northern state. Not satisfied in this body of legislation to restrict the places where free Black persons could live, to prohibit the owning of property, to forbid bringing suit against white people or testifying against them, or serving on juries in judgment over them, the state legislature in less than two generations would further codify its beliefs and fears through passage of more Black Laws on February 12, 1853. Ironically, it was the forty-fourth birthday of a Springfield, Illinois lawyer with political ambitions who would sign the Emancipation Proclamation a decade later as the sixteenth president.

The additional Black Laws were enacted by the General Assembly:

> *To prevent the immigration of free negroes into this state,* [and declaring that] *every person who shall have ¼ negro blood shall be deemed a mulatto....*[Any] *negro or mulatto slave* [shall be] *fined $100 to $500 and up to one year in prison....A ten-day proviso* [for travel] *for bond* [i.e., slave] *or free* [is granted]....[It is the authority's right] *to sell violators (negro or mulatto) at public auction* [or] *to work for and serve out said time...in servitude.* [It is granted that] *the person making complaint* [i.e., the captor of the fugitive is] *entitled to ½ of the fine, with the other ½ going to the county treasurer for the charity fund.*

Attitudes change gradually, and it's the human reality that we tend to act much of the time through our emotions rather than our reason, our fears rather than our mental faculties. Our history shows too often how decisions have been and continue to be made, with little to no thought on long-range consequence. It's the intention of this book to show how things can be different: with a change of each individual's behavior can come small changes in the direction of one's life and, by extrapolation, a change in the direction of an entire people and even of human history.

2

FOMENTING REBELLION THROUGH LAGER

If I had had to choose the place of my birth…I would have chosen a country where the right to legislate was common to all citizens—for who could know better than they what laws would most suit their living together in the same society?

—*Jean-Jacques Rousseau*, A Discourse on Inequality, *1755*

One of the attributes of Chicago leadership from the beginning has been the possession of a herculean attitude with regard to the infrastructure of the city, be it founding a city on a swamp, raising up buildings higher than originally built or reversing the flow of a river. One of Levi Boone's more inclusive accomplishments as mayor was in his vision for extended and permanent improvements in the city's drainage. Untreated sewage, standing water, rotting wooden sidewalks and decaying structures all contributed to the bacteria breeding ground that literally plagued Chicago in those early days. Boone, with a medical background, insisted on a "thorough and systematic drainage" of the entire city to combat cholera and other health hazards of nineteenth-century urban living. In addition, he championed the reconstruction of the streets "for better drainage, a smoother ride, and the longer durability of wagon and horse."

When Boone took office for the 1855 mayoral term (one year only, in those days), he also made clear his intentions to tighten the city's control of alcohol and forcefully moderate its drinking habits, which up to that time in that region of the country was a major issue. In his inaugural address, he stated that the city's charter "authorizes the Common Council to 'license, negotiate, and restrain the selling or giving away of intoxicating liquors,' and in my opinion the prohibition of the sale…is the most legitimate." New restrictions would be in place within weeks of the inauguration.

Again, John Flinn in his history claims to expose the mayor's ulterior motive: "What he intended was to drive out the small beer dealers who were scattered particularly throughout the North Side, where the Germans were in the ascendency."

The proclamation announcing the changes was made on March 17, 1855, to become effective the next day. Special officers were deputized to enforce the new ordinances, and a total of eighty men stepped up to accept the responsibility. The ordinance that increased the number of police officers also mandated that all of the city's officers were to be native-born (in a city where about half of the population was born outside the country). This was the second increase of the number of officers to keep order in a year. In 1853, construction workers walked off the job on many sites in a demand for an eight-hour Saturday workday. The owners of the company warned city officials of a disruption of peace and order, and within one week, the strike was broken with an unclear cause of its ending. The result was, in 1854, Chicago's first increase in the police force in reaction to civil disturbance.

One of the tragic features of civic authority often seems to be that particular leaders get caught off their guard when certain decisions have been made. John Hogan and Judy Brady, in their book *The Great Chicago Beer Riot*, highlight this phenomenon by showing Chicago elites attempting to address the dual "problems" of alcohol consumption and gatherings of workers in the saloons on Sundays. By enforcing the previously ignored Blue Laws already on the books to restrict certain activities on the Christian day of rest, the city hoped to restrict both beer drinking and laborers assembling outside their workplaces. This would become one of the earliest actions of municipal authority in Chicago showing its prejudice to favor business interests over the needs and desires of its working-class citizens and, most importantly, of miscalculating the popular response.

Once the effect of the Prohibitory Liquor Laws became apparent, the reaction from tavern owners was predictable. The new license fee hikes began on March 26, with the old licenses expiring on April 1. Having to pay $300 for each three-month period, from the previous $50 per year ($9,200 and $1,500, respectively, in 2021 purchasing power), alongside losing income on one of their busiest days of the week, saloon keepers rebelled. The owners remained open on the Sundays following the legislation. These offenders, predominantly of German birth, were arrested, with their trial dates set to begin on April 21.

Hogan and Brady, in their previously referenced book, give excellent detail as to the actual downtown fighting on the weekend of the twenty-first, near the courthouse at Randolph and Clark Streets, as Germans from the north side attempted an armed rescue of the imprisoned tavern owners. The mayor ordered the bridge to be turned at Clark Street over the river at what is presently Wacker Drive (this swivel construction predated the modern raised bridge design) so as to prevent more protestors from crossing into downtown. It was the first use of a bridge against citizens in protest, and the precursor to the latest use of them during the George Floyd protests and the rioting in 2020.

Boone called up four of the seven local militia units and hired Allan Pinkerton and his detectives to join the volunteers and officers, over two hundred in all. In the ensuing violence of street fighting, it was reported that shouts of "Shoot the police" and "Pick out the stars" came from the crowds gathered for the confrontation. When all had been quieted, over sixty arrests had been made and one protestor killed.

As is typical in the urban experience, once a situation has exploded in violence, it becomes apparent that memories about what happened become foggy. In Chicago, in the aftermath of the violence on that April weekend in 1855, blame was placed on the shoulders of the already-burdened immigrants. The Wentworth-owned *Chicago Democrat* editorialized: "[The riot,] we have learned was only an extraordinary row; got up by persons not generally known in our city, a few of them Frenchmen, a few Italians, a few Germans, and a few American loafers generally." The *Free West*, in an article titled "Terrible Riot in Chicago," concurred: "The supremacy of righteous and just laws has been maintained in Chicago. The rummies and foreign rowdies have learned that they cannot defy the sober community and the legal authorities of the city."

Within a week of the riot, the city council voted 8–7 for a new organization that would become the modern-day Chicago Police Department. This new body would taint the attitudes of the largely German north siders against the police into the next century. At the same time, newly appointed head of the police department Cyrus Parker Bradley acted on the growing attitudes of civil authority against the immigrant classes. Throughout the remainder of the year, arrests rose, many for public intoxication, with the Irish (newly arrived and poorest) accounting for over 65 percent of those charged, while only accounting for 20 percent of Chicago's population at that time.

The city's executives, however, did have the ability to admit partial defeat: they sensed a pushback from voters regarding the early prohibition

May Day 2014 at the Haymarket Memorial in Chicago's West Loop neighborhood. *Courtesy of the author.*

movement and did back down on its draconian and punitive ordinances governing alcohol. The ban on taverns' Sunday opening was lifted, and the licensing fee went from the original $300 increase to $100 as support for the restrictions lost momentum in the city as well as throughout Cook County.

Again, the hand wringing and shoulder shrugging of those in power betray their genuine shock (or maybe denial and naiveté) when situations they assume are under control suddenly degenerate into chaos. History and the human experience are filled with "What ifs?"

What if civic authority had publicly debated a proposal for the Prohibitory Liquor Law before it had been codified? What if saloon owners had been brought into the discussion?

What if the needs of the growing ranks of foreign-born workers had been addressed in the workplace by their employers as they arose? What if the fears of those supporting the growing temperance movement were articulated with less emotion and more reasoned debate? What if a show of rational discourse was the first choice, rather than a show of raw force?

Lesson no. 1 in the School of Hard Knocks should be "Don't repeat the mistakes of the past: Do the different."

While the 1855 Lager Beer Riot is seen as of slightly lesser consequence than what was to come in the following three generations in Chicago, the incident could have provided politicians a template for future behavior and policy. This genuine reassessment might have given them some pause in regard to the growing tensions and issues brought on by fire, a rising immigrant population that showed no sign of abating, a large migration of freed human beings into the city from two centuries of slavery and an unstoppable flexing of muscle from the newborn labor movement. Chicago could have become a model city, a glowing city, in fact and in name in these early days, lighting a path to social harmony for the rest of the country as it teetered on the ledge and stared into the chasm of civil war.

3

A CITY IGNITED

I sang about Anchises' son, the just
Aeneas, pious, peerless. When proud Troy
was burned to ashes, ashes turned to dust
which he shook off his feet, that marvelous boy.
He did what any decent hero must:
Set sail. But you, you turn back. Tell me why.
Why not press on to the delightful peak?
The root cause of all joy is in the sky.

—*Dante Alighieri,* The Divine Comedy: Inferno,
first canto, fourteenth century

Carl Smith, in the introduction to his *Urban Disorder and the Shape of Belief,* states that the role of the historian is to keep objectivity at the front of any study of the past.

While I cannot withhold judgement in many instances where I think it is vital to responsible and meaningful inquiry, I think that it would be hypocritical a century and more later to feign surprise that very few individuals were able to see beyond their interests....Like all of us, they were not simply looking for ways in which to weather a particular moment, but for a view of the world in which they could imaginatively live.

True as this may be, it is the chief focus of this work to home in on several events in Chicago's past and, like in a fencing match, thrust for the target to point at what could have been done differently in order that while trudging through our present, we might mark a path forward for future generations to model rather than to scorn.

The Great Chicago Fire of 1871 resulted in one of the greatest resurrection stories of the world's countless urban disasters. The Second City that rose from the ashes of the first one is certainly an amazing feat of near-biblical proportions. It's been a source of pride to the city and its people, on the verge of its third century. It would be redundant (and off topic for this study) to focus on the tragedy and the resilience of the people in rebuilding from the devastation. It is more to the point of this work to look at the effects of the tragedy just days after rains doused the flames as well as in the months and years of rebuilding that followed.

The experience of the fire showed great courage and selfless action of thousands of people from all economic levels who were in the midst of the disaster. For a brief period, Chicagoans were equal: most citizens were in mortal peril or thought they were; over 100,000 (about one-third of the city's population at the time) would be homeless after the three days of burning had died out; and all lived in the vast unknown of the ashes in that first week afterward. Journalists who reported their firsthand experiences are numerous, as are the works of countless photographers who chronicled the physical aftermath. These are the reliable sources that most historians have used to archive the events.

Quickly, though, other accounts of the fire began to be composed—and invented. Partly out of the need to publish news alongside pleas for speedy relief, as well as from twisted, self-serving desire to profit from the national and international appetite for sensationalism, pamphleteers used their printing power to put out anything and everything about the fire. It was in this manner that further damage was inflicted on immigrants. Stories of crazed ruffians burning the city and "disgracing" girls and women were plentiful, as were stories of "good citizens" keeping guard over the city against the vandals who would seek to profit from the chaos. These tales usually ended with a rallying cry for law and order that even went so far as to hold up lynching as the best way to achieve security. Vigilantism thrived at this time but never reached the levels it was to attain in the post–Civil War South through de facto legalized lynchings of African Americans well into the twentieth century.

The classic tale of the cow kicking over the lantern in Mrs. O'Leary's barn on October 8, 1871, may have been the invention of a pamphleteer, but it does expose the very real and prevailing anti-immigrant attitude of the city at that time. While the fire did begin in the largely Irish section of the south side—and may have been ignited on the property of Catherine and Patrick O'Leary—contemporary accounts of the fire and its aftermath focused on the drunkenness, criminal bent and questionable political views of the large numbers of the ethnic poor that lurked amid the smoking embers.

Smith's *Urban Disorder* chronicles the nearly immediate abrogation of civil order to that of the "Democracy of the Hour" that caused Chicagoans of all social classes to huddle together for their physical well-being along the lakeshore. A nineteenth-century writer, Alfred Andreas, sharpened his quill to stab at the real catastrophe, or at least the one he envisioned, and it wasn't the inferno consuming the city:

> *Human creatures…*[like] *maddened animals delicate and refined women, pure and innocent children…young girls, whose artless lives were unfamiliar with even the name of crime…men of well-ordered lives and Christian minds* [found themselves with] *brutes in human form, who were not only ready to do acts of crime, but whose polluting wickedness was rank, and cast-off prison fumes upon the air….Could all the powers of hell devise a keener form of anguish?*

The perceived real tragedy had been exposed, and the breakdown of the social order would be the impetus for immediate address by the city fathers. Not simply were building codes revised from wooden structures to brick and a professional fire department established, but the reassertion of the neatly-defined class consciousness would restore order to the once and future sprawling city as well.

Adding to fears of the demise of society, the destruction of sections of the French capital six months earlier after the two-month standoff of the Paris Commune fueled passions in Chicago regarding political violence. No proof of sabotage has ever been brought out through responsible study over the 150 years since the fire, but at the time it was believed to be very probable that the nefarious and *foreign* Communards in Chicago had something to do with the inferno. The American scapegoating of political radicals follows the typical pattern of monarchs, dictators and other demagogues who have seen challenges to the established order as evil. This tactic would be repeated several times up to and including the summer of 2020.

The deportation of members of the Industrial Workers of the World (IWW or "Wobblies") in 1913. *Courtesy of the Chicago History Museum (i182677_001_pm).*

The altar had already been prepared for the sacrificial offering of the working class to the god Status Quo by the time the city's rebuilding began to be planned. By that first winter's approach just weeks after the fire, the relief money that was beginning to arrive almost immediately after the fire was distributed through the Chicago Relief and Aid Society. Of the nearly $5 million (over $100 billion in 2021 purchasing power), about $4.4 million was given out in direct relief to businesses and citizens. Now, while the accounts of the activity of this group are open for study, and while there is solid proof that the money was not squandered, the method of the distribution of funds demonstrates the narrow views of the ruling class.

Businesses were favored to receive much of the money in an Industrial Age version of the trickle-down theory, made infamous by President Ronald Reagan a century later: recovery happens quickly when money is received metaphorically into the top glasses of the economic pyramid (business interests and the propertied class) and then trickles down to all the other glasses below (the working class and the poor). As this author observed in a previous work, *Chicago Socialism: The People's History*, while the theory sounds plausible, the ugly reality has yet to be contradicted: the wealth poured into the top glasses (the top hats of the wealthy, metaphorically speaking) never gets down to the working "glasses" because the vessels at the top continue to get larger.

So it seemed to the general population that had no business interests outside their own employment. The Relief and Aid Society, in its final accounting in 1874, stated that it offered

> *such temporary help to the deserving poor…to tide them over those hard places in life which single handed and alone they are unequal to—discontinuing at the earliest moment that it is possible for them to provide for themselves, thus guarding carefully against encouraging a feeling of dependence upon the society.*

The aid was essential to the recovery of everyone in the city, but the dispensers of that relief kept up the front of we and they instead of the grand We who were all suffering and in need of some kind of relief. As months passed and the second winter after the fire approached, the unity of the disaster had dissipated to almost nonexistence. What was seen as stalled distribution of the relief fund was exacerbated by a national economic depression, rising unemployment throughout the country and the anticipation of the midwestern winter.

On December 21, 1872, needy citizens gathered outside the downtown offices of the Relief and Aid Society on Clark and Randolph Streets in what would be called the Bread Riot. On Mayor Joseph Medill's order, police ushered the crowd down Randolph Street, westward, to the LaSalle Street Tunnel, under the Chicago River, that had served as a main downtown escape route during the fire. This time, the tunnel would serve the nefarious purpose of quelling the restless population into submission as officers used clubs to turn the people away from the center of the city.

Again, city officials played the dumb card and failed to understand the desperation of people who were nothing of the vagrant, loafer or anarchist classes to which they were accused of belonging. They were the unemployed, the hungry and desperate who felt they were entitled to that which had been promised to all. Even after the embers of this post-fire incident cooled, those in office continued their seemingly programmed actions of governance: tell the people what they want, since *we* are the ones equipped to steer the conversation—or, more accurately, the monologue.

What could have been done differently? To begin with, the relief efforts could have followed a different path had the thinking been altered, with the old mentality left to burn away with the old city. One can hope that our best can rise up from tragedy. For a brief period, the city knew a different reality: the great egalitarian, fire, bestowed its democracy on everyone with relative equality. To continue along this vein, the city as a whole, full of an embattled people with similar experiences of loss, could have sought solace as well as action. Representatives from all groups and from all wards could have eased the burden of the individual and been themselves given a sense of ownership that had not existed in the city before the fire. Had city officials opened discussion of proposed new fire codes, shown the benefits of building a city of brick rather than wood and creatively pursued the best ways to help all citizens pay for the changes in city ordinances as they related to such building code amendments, positive conditions might have grown with a vibrancy of civic activity and led to a radically different Second City than the one that actually rose up.

Sadly, the history that played out was full of the same attitudes, fears, prejudices and actions of the few. Well-intentioned as they may have been, these elites failed once again to understand the need for inclusion and of questioning preconceived stereotypes. With the road to rebuilding already paved, it became the latest in the historical train of the same; the adage that history repeats itself would continue along the same track.

But a restless population, a rising voice as it were, had already made itself heard, albeit from a distance and in a low decibel. All the talking and planning of the optimate class, those best people chosen to govern, would be silenced once again, but then spew louder and be cowed into silence again and again over the next thirty years, to shout even louder again and again in the face of what would become the growing march of the Chicago worker. They would begin to learn, albeit with resistance and more bloodshed, how to listen differently.

4

LABOR'S LABOR PAINS
AND THE BIRTH OF DEFIANCE

For without this right to the free use of [land, tools and the fruits of one's own labor], *the pursuit of happiness, the enjoyment of liberty and life itself are hollow mockeries. Hence the employment of any and all means are justifiable in obtaining them, even to a forceable violent revolution....* [Armed workers], *thus being in a position to argue* [their] *case, the final compact might possibly be achieved by very little violence.*
—*Lucy Parsons, 1883*

ELECTION BLUES REAP MUCH RED

By the time Lucy Parsons spoke these words, she and her husband, Albert, were among the recognized leadership of the burgeoning groups of anarcho-socialists in Chicago. In the fifteen years that followed the Great Fire, Chicago and the nation would witness the growth of the modern labor movement, following in many ways the rise of the working classes in industrial yet still monarchical Europe as well as the slow awakening of the peasantry in tsarist Russia.

And with the violent repression of workers by the great powers throughout the Old World since 1848 would come great imitation by leaders in the New World—reaction against the young muscle of labor in most urban centers in the United States. It's interesting to observe the selectivity of this imitation on the part of industrialists and politicians in this country: what is foreign is deemed worthy of notice and imitation only in this area by American power-wielders when it comes to fossilized attitudes of the enthroned who cling to power with a dying grip.

Lucy and Albert Parsons would abandon the idea of radical change through the ballot box after the 1877, 1879 and 1881 municipal elections showed rampant criminality centered on both Democrats and Republicans. The now-famous adage "Vote early and often" was coined during the 1877 contest by the *Chicago Daily News* after its favored candidate, Republican mayor Monroe Heath, won reelection against the apparently more crooked (at least according to the Republicans) Democrat Perry Smith. Ballot box stuffing, ward committeemen strong-arming voters, suppression of the Black vote in the First and Third Wards and bribery at all levels would continue to plague Chicago like the cholera that the city battled in its earliest days.

Though election reforms were enacted beginning in 1883, the "pay to play" politics that would be a staple in Chicago and Illinois into the next century and well beyond remained entrenched. So much so did the ruling elite think itself untouchable, it could unashamedly put forth safe reforms to ensure that its infamy would continue. If any single group is to bear a great share of responsibility for the rise of nineteenth-century political violence in Chicago, it is this caste of politicians and unelected power-wielders that eventually forced the leadership of the Socialistic Labor Party closer to the anarchist camp, away from a more intellectual/philosophical anarchy of no coercive government over individuals, to a more revolutionary and immediate destructive angle of social change through bomb and gun.

In 1878, the Socialistic Labor Party could still boast a solid platform of social reforms via the conventional electoral process: full voting rights for women (only attained by the two major parties in 1920), an end to child labor (only attained by the two major parties in 1937) and an eight-hour cap on the workday (only attained by the two major parties in 1937). The Socialist Party saw its strongest showing in 1879 when three of its candidates won seats in the city council and four state legislative seats in Springfield; the socialist mayoral candidate garnered 20 percent of the votes cast, and the party witnessed a voter turnout that exceeded one thousand votes each in six out of the twenty wards. This "Red Wave" was to be the first and last great splash until the 2019 municipal elections that saw six socialist candidates take seats in the city council chambers. The party would splinter from 1881 onward, and national and international fears of anarchist revolution would drain it of a good portion of its popular support after the 1886 Haymarket bombing.

After the Civil War, the wealth gap widened between rich and poor in urban and rural areas and among those who had recently been enslavers and the recently emancipated. The five-year conflict had reaped riches for those in the growing clothing manufacturing industry, in food production and in large-scale farming; at the same time, it destroyed cities and left hundreds of thousands of acres of farmland blood-soaked and scarred. Some profited, and many others suffered more in the aftermath of the war.

Marshall Field, Philip Armour and the aforementioned McCormick brothers, among others, all found their greatest fortunes in Chicago after the war, polishing them to a blinding shimmer throughout the so-called Gilded Age of the late nineteenth century. Their rise necessitated others' demise— or, more to the point, the keeping down of the working class that provided the fuel for the industrialists' upward thrust. The story of the haves and have-nots would turn another page in cities and farms alike, as well as take on a new angle and hue in the former Confederacy.

According to the 1860 U.S. Census, over 3.5 million human beings were classified as slaves. They would find themselves emancipated in 1863 and in April 1865 released into a new existence that in many ways differed little from their former lives. While many of the enslavers received reparations payments from the federal government as early as 1862, when Abraham Lincoln signed the District of Columbia Emancipation Act ($300 for each slave who had been freed in the capital, in keeping with the Fifth Amendment's mandate of "just compensation" for government seizure of the "private assets" of the enslaver [about $8,000 in 2021 purchasing power]), no federal or state payout in any noteworthy form has ever been given to those who were enslaved.

Even the grand gesture of General William Tecumseh Sherman, as he marched and incinerated great swaths of Georgia, was hollow. He saw the giving of captured southern lands (the famous "forty acres and a mule") to those who formerly were held captive there as a solution to their aimless wandering in the wake of his March to the Sea. A grand gesture—however, it was nullified by President Andrew Johnson after Lincoln's assassination, and the newly freed were expelled from the land so as to restore the commandeered property back to the former enslaving population. Even the territory of the Jeffersonian land grab known as the Louisiana Purchase, acquired from the Napoleonic imperialists, and other lands belonging to the original Natives dwelling on the continent were made the exclusive booty of white settlers and out of the reach of the formerly enslaved and the original dwellers of the land.

As cannons cooled across the once-divided nation, old tensions strained the reunification of the states in the decade following the war. In one of the most blatant manipulations of the Constitution, the aftermath of the 1876 presidential election witnessed Democrats and Republicans uniting in assuring the victory of Rutherford B. Hayes over Samuel Tilden in the first decision given to the winner of the electoral votes over the candidate with an absolute majority of the popular vote total: Democrats in the southern states promised their electoral votes for Republican Hayes in exchange for the withdrawal of federal troops of the Reconstruction effort from the defeated, Democratic-controlled former Confederacy. Once Hayes was declared the nineteenth president, he kept the smoke-filled backroom promise and pulled the occupying army from the South. This action of power-grubbing, self-centered political expediency paved the road for apartheid to be the law of the land in the southern states, and it lasted well into the latter half of the twentieth century.

The Great Upheaval of 1877

Almost as divine retribution for their electoral treachery fit for a Greek epic, Hayes and the political elites of both capitalist parties, before Hayes's first year in office was completed, were all thrust into the midst of a clash that could have resulted in either a second revolution or another civil war, right in the cannon treads of the last conflict. One or the other could have happened, and it would have been rooted in the growing inequity between capital and labor.

Even at this point, however, there was still the hope that laborers could advocate for a more just society in the workplace through peaceful means. The newly sprawled system of railroads across the country provided the impetus for the first postwar test of the stamina of workers. But that was not to be: beginning in the fall of 1876, during yet another economic depression, owners of the Baltimore and Ohio Railroad (the B&O) implemented the third wage cut in a year (this one was a 20 percent slash of wages) for all workers, with no announcement or evidence of cuts to the executives in the company or of dividends to shareholders.

The railroad employees in Martinsville, West Virginia, were the first to walk out on July 14, 1877, followed by thousands of others from Philadelphia to St. Louis and all points in between. According to John Flinn, in his 1887 police history, "The spirit of the riot, like some spectral courier of a dreadful epidemic, was advancing westwardly, and conquering as it came." Governors from West Virginia to Missouri called out their state militias and the National Guard. Within the first few days, the walkouts turned violent, with most of the outbreaks occurring in Pittsburg and Chicago. In his book *1877: Year of Violence*, Robert V. Bruce recounts the destruction of railway yards, trains and buildings along with attacks against armories. When the Pittsburg wing of the state guard refused to fire on the striking workers, the governor called on Philadelphians to take up arms and move into Pittsburg. A violent confrontation was avoided, but the situation illustrates the level of tension as well as the splits in sympathies in the country.

Chicago was particularly violent in the latter part of the two-week July revolt. From the twenty-fourth to the twenty-eighth, railway workers, lumberers, meatpackers, garment workers—men, women and children (the U.S. Census, until 1940, defined *wage earner* as ten years old and older)—of the Second City walked away from their jobs in solidarity with their fellow wage slaves in the east. The Parsonses, while still clinging weakly to the hope of change through the ballot, took the lead with fiery speeches, as well as at rallies and parades—and took the brunt of the blame for the violence that ensued. Again, historian and contemporary witness of the events John Flinn observed:

> *Discontent was general among the wage classes. Socialism had been planted here, and it grew luxuriantly in the soil so well-prepared for it. There were socialistic societies by the hundred, which held regular meetings throughout the city, and great mass meetings occasionally on Market Street* [present-day Wacker Drive, at the Lyric Opera], *the Haymarket* [in West Loop on Randolph Street], *or the lake shore* [Ogden's Grove]. *The grievances of the wage-workers were palpable and great. Things could not very well look more hopeless for them. The demagogue* [Albert Parsons] *was in his glory, and he demanded war upon capital, vengeance upon the "privileged classes." A great unemployed labor demonstration had paraded the streets. Thousands of poorly clad, hungry looking men were in line. A banner with the startling device "Bread or Blood."*

Flinn's account covers the action of city officials: the mayor oversaw that "all the bridges leading to the West Side were swung [to stand parallel with the river thereby prohibiting people from crossing the river as was first done in 1855], the tunnels were guarded, and armed men patrolled the downtown streets." In one instance, he cites the action of one rioter who "swung the Halsted Street bridge (near Goose Island) to prohibit the advance of police and federal troops." This appears to be the only time when a protestor used a bridge against civil authority in Chicago.

Over the course of these days, there would be several clashes of striking workers against the police, the Illinois National Guard and federal troops, fresh from the western battlefields that used to be home to the Native Americans. The bloodiest conflict was on Halsted, between 16th and 18th Streets, in what would be known as the Battle of the Viaduct. This two-day fight would be the cap of the violence in Chicago that would tally twenty deaths out of the total one hundred who died across the country in the weeks of the strike.

The fearmongering continued in the collective memory. Flinn would perpetuate the stereotype and fan the flames in his account:

> *Hundreds of those who shouted for higher wages and better treatment were vagabonds.…Hundreds were confirmed criminals, hundreds were professional thieves. But the most dangerous element of all were the foreigners who belonged to the communistic societies and who were endeavoring to bring about a period of the blackest anarchy.*

Again, there was no reflection on the root causes of the upheaval either nationally or in Chicago. There were reasons why the socialist message was so desirable to particular groups of people, and those reasons were consistently being ignored by those in positions of authority. Blame was placed on the working class and on labor leaders, socialists, communists and anyone else who rose to speak on behalf of improving the equitable distribution of the fruits of human labor. And again, politicians at the federal, state and local levels defended the railway corporations, the industrialists who felt the pinch of the strike and the governors who looked to the White House for protections against the grumbling masses. Nowhere except in the socialistic circles was there any discussion about monopolies, robber barons, corporate greed, overextension of the military or the plight of the urban poor. And nowhere would there be such smoldering anger as in these same circles of mass discontent.

And history seems to be repeating again in the wake of what has been called the Great Resignation following the 2020 worldwide lockdown. The attitude that enough is enough has been repeated and screamed in the walkout of a large portion of the working class, especially in the service industries

An example of a pipe bomb similar to ones made in the 1880s and a "czar bomb," similar to the one thrown at the end of the Haymarket rally on May 4, 1886. *Courtesy of the Chicago History Museum.*

and what many feel are the dead-end white-collar jobs. But as has become the expected tactic of the ruling class, blame for the sluggish recovery and difficulty in filling old jobs has been again placed on the shoulders of the hourly wage slaves. The expectation was that "they" would come back to the same drudgery for the same hourly pay, inconsistent health coverage and thanklessness from boss and customer so that "we" could get back to normal. And it didn't play out that way—the level of frustration, fear and overall fed-upness of workers rose with feet in the grand walkout that is still reverberating today.

WARNINGS UNHEEDED AND SOCIAL ORDER UNHINGED

The post-election alleged reforms of 1880s Chicago were met with the abandonment that was to curse the city and nation over the next five years and beyond. The business-as-usual attitudes of the city council and mayors showed workers that their lot was not likely to improve in the near future. By 1885, strikes, rallies and more violence had erupted again. Thanksgiving Day marches up and down Prairie Avenue around 21st Street, the nineteenth century's Gold Coast, in 1884 and 1885 highlighted workers' desires for "Work or Bread," as per the reports disseminated from the city's newspapers. The McCormick Reaper Works, having mourned the 1884 death of patriarch and relative labor liberal Cyrus, came under the leadership of his eldest son, Cyrus Jr., who was less a friend of the worker and witnessed the first of several strikes beginning in 1885. The Parsonses organized protest rallies against the dedication of the Board of Trade building at Jackson and LaSalle Streets that April. Minimal violence there, a strong police presence and the retreat of the protestors led officials to ignore the firebrand speeches of the leaders that were given and were to appear in the papers over the next several days.

An eruption would occur at the end of June 1885, which again gave leaders an opportunity to reflect on and try to resolve the ongoing tensions

The Laws are made to be enforced.
The Laws are made to be enforced.
The Laws are made to be enforced.
The Laws are made to be enforced.
The Laws are mad

From a political cartoon around the turn of the century (nineteenth to twentieth). *Courtesy of the Newberry Library.*

of the laboring classes. Employees of the West Division Street Railway Company, the precursor to the Chicago Transit Authority, along with citizens of the city were informed of both wage cuts of the workers on the line as well as fare increases to the riders. And yet again, there was no addressing of salary cuts for those in management. Added to this was the news that the committee of workers who sought arbitration with the company had been fired.

In the ensuing week of the strike, workers and customers rallied together to disconnect horses from the streetcars, upend tracks and mock the labor-friendly Mayor Carter Harrison, who had to go out to meet with the crowds while dodging bricks. Congressman Frank Lawlor tried to introduce a bill that would cancel the streetcar company's charter with Chicago but was unsuccessful. The city's newspapers reported on the violence, blamed "roughs, socialists, thieves, and foolish respectable people" and quoted the safe, law and order line of police superintendent Austin J. Doyle: "If citizens would obey the law, there would be no trouble."

Numerous accounts in Chicago's newspapers, and cited by Flinn, had to admit how out of hand the situation had gotten as they documented several instances of violence by civil authority against workers who were not part of the strike. Simply doing their jobs, employees of a construction company laying pipe along the street were beaten by police. This oft-enemy of labor, the mainstream press at the time, even recorded beatings by the civil authorities of a seventeen-year-old girl and a man of seventy who happened to be walking along the sidewalk in one of the troubled areas.

By the middle of July, tensions were easing, and the streetcars were running again; the president of the company, J. Russell Jones, promised to look into the cases of the discharged workers, and both sides agreed to submit any future grievances to arbitration (actually a revolutionary concept at the time). However, as with most things human, there was a vast difference of interpretation: Lucy Parsons was quoted in the *Chicago Daily Tribune* saying that "the strike was a comic opera with three acts, the last one, the settlement, being a huge farce." This divergent view helps describe why the city was caught off guard in less than a year when a bomb was thrown near Haymarket Square.

The events of the summer appeared to have borne fruit regarding organized labor: by the end of the year, workers at the McCormick Reaper Works plant had received a guarantee that no one would be discharged because of organizing. However, Flinn's *History* testifies to something of a change of plan: "It [the guarantee of non-punitive action against organizers] had been forcibly extorted [in 1885] and the company, finding itself in a position to resist [in 1886] now decided to throw off the yoke and resume its independence." The typical double standard was at work: a company could lure workers into a state of ease, for the company's own security, then later snap its jaws against those who actively organized fellow workers for the benefit and security of those same workers.

The winter of 1885–86 saw more tensions between owners of business and workers. Another strike at the McCormick plant had intensified in February alongside numerous walkouts around the city of carpenters, bricklayers and garment workers over the ensuing weeks. Labor organizers throughout the country planned for a national strike in support of the 8-Hour Workday Movement to begin on Saturday, May 1. It was to be the first time that May Day was taken as Labor Day, which to this day is still recognized as International Workers Day, except in the United States and a

Workers standing outside a furniture store on the eve of the first nationwide strike for the eight-hour workday, April 30, 1886. *Courtesy of the Chicago History Museum (i020069)*.

handful of other holdout countries. There was still time on the part of the ruling class to meet the growing push of labor and embrace it as the main vehicle to social harmony.

But once again, choosing fear over reason, industrialists and politicians reacted against what they interpreted as troublemaking by an elite few. They were joined by several labor leaders in the more conservative wings of the worker movement who saw the various branches of socialists usurping the eight-hour efforts and feared extremist elements using the general movement for a reduction of the workday as a springboard for something more revolutionary.

In any event, the nationwide strike began on May 1 with an estimated strength of sixty to eighty thousand men, women and children nationwide walking off their jobs on that first day of the strike, with others following them over the next three days. Chicagoans made up at least a quarter of the national total. Parades, rallies and clear skies over the city resulting from the work stoppage marked the weekend and that Monday/Tuesday. A few businesses had already begun to grant concessions to their workers by offering a Saturday half day, some modified hours of the work week and modest pay increases.

It seemed to many that this show of strength would actually introduce a new era of capital/labor harmony. But again, it was a fleeting hope: the more radical members of the labor movement, the uneasy anarcho-socialist groups in the city and the jittery city authorities were poised and ready for something less utopian. On the afternoon of Monday, May 3, striking workers gathered in a field across from an entrance to the McCormick plant in an effort to taunt the strikebreakers (scabs) into abandoning their undermining of the strike. Following the pattern of civil disturbance, it's unclear who started what, but the result was violence: rocks were thrown, shots fired, police on site fired and were fired on (or vice versa), one worker was killed, several others were wounded and, most importantly, the ire of the people was again ignited.

August Spies and others organized a protest rally for the next night in Haymarket Square; Lucy and Albert Parsons would meet them on the night of the fourth. During the final of three speeches that evening, the weather began to turn as the final speaker, Samuel Fielden, wrapped up his words. About 160 police officers from the Des Plaines Street station marched the half block to the speakers' wagon and ordered the meeting to end. A bomb was thrown in the midst of the phalanx of officers, of which a total of eight died and several were injured along with an undetermined number of civilians. The ensuing gunfighting lasted several minutes before the street was cleared and the roundup of suspects began. In the course of the next several days, under martial law, known socialists (most with German names) were arrested, evidence was acquired without warrants and the trial of the Haymarket Eight would capture worldwide attention for the next several months.

Hundreds of thousands of pages have been written about the bombing, trials, executions and exonerations related to the Haymarket Affair. The details are for a reader's or student's study outside this work. But suffice it to say that the purposes of the city, the state's attorney and judge/jury were to protect the law and order of society. In the words of Julius Grinnell, chief prosecutor, "Anarchy is on trial here." It was a clear target that provided civil authority the wherewithal to seal the rights of the propertied few over the needs of the working class, under the guise of saving society from the beast, anarchy (anarchy being defined widely as anything out of step with keeping those in power in power).

Few outside the socialist groups saw the double standard of government and business leaders condemning their attempt to push the labor movement in a more radical direction while not criticizing the rapid industrialization in the middle of the century that had ushered in the massive suffering of workers that they sought to address. And few in the anarchist wing of socialists would have argued with John Flinn as he reflected on the bombing a year later that "the destruction of the legal authorities of the state and country [was the goal, along with] a complete revolution of the existing order." This was precisely the goal. The need for violent change had been brought about by the blatant and consistent exclusion of the powerless citizenry from the electoral process in Chicago, other cities and the nation as a whole. It was a new age, and those holding the scepter failed to see, or refused to face, the changes that were already being ushered in.

The men, older and younger, who held power through property and controlled the ballot box were of the same cut and color: they were the bearded (no women), well-fed (a late nineteenth-century symbol of abundance), well-dressed, white, university-educated and staid-in-their-worldview individuals who, in this view, assumed they knew what was best for society. These were the elected officials and judges sitting in courtrooms of cities and states, all the way to the U.S. Supreme Court. This group of rulers was unwilling to or simply incapable of seeing that the social

The Supreme Court under Chief Justice Melville Fuller, from the 1880s; many of these justices decided the *In Re: Debs* and *Plessy v. Ferguson* cases in the 1890s.

order had failed to keep pace (or order) with the astronomical growth of industry, leaving masses on the lower rungs dangling.

The principles of a cultural Darwinism, a justification of the survival of the fittest businesses and nations, seeped into the minds of corporate leaders hellbent on constructing an unrestrained and ironclad capitalism alongside empire-dreaming heads of state both homegrown and overseas. Again, these Optimates, the best people, those assumed to be fittest to lead, failed to understand anything outside the gilded world. They did not understand the significance of Karl Marx's warning of the alienation of workers from their work, from their co-workers and from themselves. In so failing to understand, businessmen and politicians continued to repeat their own mistakes as well as those of their predecessors.

In less than a decade after four of the Haymarket convicted were executed, the nation would get yet another chance to rectify the gross inequities brought on by the juggernaut, capital, steamrolling across the country. The powerful Chicago railroad magnate George Pullman squared off in the eyes of the nation with the bookish labor leader and socialist Eugene Debs in yet another struggle between the rights of property owners and those of the worker. Had either American businessmen or politicians accepted basic principles from their elders in the European industrial community as to what *not* to do regarding the growing strength of the working class, many lessons could have been learned and some trouble could have been avoided.

But what has plagued this country for more than two and a half centuries of its existence is a toxic amount of American exceptionalism that has been allowed to seep into the nation's psyche. In 1887, John Flinn stated it with clarity:

> *It may be claimed here that European customs have nothing whatever to do with the arrangement of affairs in this country; that we are not now, and never have been guided by them, and that we never will permit European ideas to control, or even enter into our method of doing things....Were the capitalists, the employers, of the United States to take as readily and as lovingly to the teachings of European capitalists and employers, as the workingmen of this country do to the teachings of newly-arrived immigrants* [read "anarcho-socialism"]...*then this would be a land of misery.*

The ignorance of this view hindered the powerholders in their attempts to harness the growing energy and impatience of laborers as the Industrial Age

THE VANGUARD OF ANARCHY.

The *Harper's Weekly* lampooning of Eugene Debs as the harbinger of anarchy as he took the lead in the Pullman strike in 1894. *Courtesy of the Chicago History Museum (i182676_pm).*

steamed ahead, obscene wealth and desperate poverty on a collision course across the ever-expanding nation.

Jane Addams, founder of Chicago's early settlement organization Hull-House, noted a completely different phenomenon regarding what is American and what is foreign as she reflected on her abolitionist father's reaction to the news of the death of the Italian patriot Giuseppe Mazzini, whom her father had never met, in 1872:

> *A sense of the genuine relationship which may exist between men who share large hopes and like desires, even though they may differ in nationality, language, and creed; that those things count for absolutely nothing between groups of men who are trying to abolish slavery in America or to throw off Hapsburg oppression in Italy.*

It's difficult, if not impossible, to see oneself or one's own people as exceptional with a worldview that encompasses the entire planet of fellow human beings as citizens of the same people. Books of this nature would not need to be written if this were the case.

5

REASON, RACE AND RAW POWER

I had felt that the protection of the law itself extended to the most unpopular citizen was the only reply to the anarchistic argument, to the effect that this moment of panic [the 1901 assassination of President William McKinley] *revealed the truth of their theory of government; that the custodians of law and order have become the government itself quite as the armed men hired by the medieval guilds to protect them in the peaceful pursuit of their avocations through sheer possession of arms finally made themselves rulers of the city.*
—*Jane Addams,* Twenty Years at Hull-House, *1910*

BLOOD FROM A TURNIP: YOU MAKE HOW MUCH... I MEAN, HOW LITTLE?

A woman from Cedarville, Illinois, Jane Addams, was to become yet another leader in the United States who, while witnessing the tarnishing of the Gilded Age at the close of the nineteenth century, worked to provide peaceful transitions to a new era of social harmony. She set up the first settlement houses in the Midwest in 1889 as a refuge for the growing immigrant population in Chicago before and after the turn of the century. She worked to put a human face on the growing wretchedness with which newcomers had to contend at a time when ruling voices were dehumanizing the growing economic forces and furthering the objectification and alienation of the worker.

Just one week after the Haymarket bombing of May 4, the U.S. Supreme Court decided in favor of the Southern Pacific Railroad Company's claim against Santa Clara County, California, stating that the railroad was exempt from a tax levied against it: while not written in words, the decision upheld the corporation's right to the Equal Protections clause of the Fourteenth Amendment. While not a "natural person," the railroad received the same protections a citizen was guaranteed. The constitutional protection that granted basic rights to citizens who had been freed from slavery by the Thirteenth Amendment was now being used to confer the same status on growing industrial conglomerates. The court would upend that same Fourteenth Amendment two more times in the next ten years: first, with its infamous 1895 judgment *In Re: Debs*, favoring the Pullman Palace Car Company, which had, with the aid of the federal government, crushed a nationwide strike the year before; and second, through the *Plessy v. Ferguson* decision codifying segregation in 1896.

In 1893, following the same corporate pattern as in the past, the Pullman Company ordered wage cuts of its employees and residents of the company village of Pullmantown following an economic depression that would last from 1893 to 1897. George Pullman, the creator of the town for his workers that bore his name, insisted that the cuts were necessary, that the company's profits were down, indeed a losing proposition at the time, he insisted, and that no cuts in rents or utilities were possible. However, according to the report of the 1895 federal Strike Commission that would be established in the wake of the Pullman strike, company profits from July 1, 1893, to the same date in 1894 allowed the company to pay out dividends to its shareholders of $2.5 million in 1893 and $2.8 million in 1894 ($74 million and $86 million, respectively, in 2021 purchasing power). At the same time, the total amount paid for wages fell from $7 million to $4 million (from $208 million to $119 million in 2021 purchasing power).

By the beginning of 1894, unrest throughout the country had reached levels that were reminiscent of the Great Upheaval of 1877. The first March on Washington was organized in the spring of 1894 in Ohio by businessman Jacob Coxey. In addition to other "industrial armies from the west," Chicago would be the starting point of another march that May Day demanding work on its way to the nation's capital. The thrust of the movement was to pressure the federal government to stimulate the economy through massive public works programs, most particularly in the system of roads throughout the country. This is yet another example of those who were excluded from the decision-making and problem-solving processes proposing solutions that are ignored in their own day, yet are usurped as the brainchild of the capitalist parties generations later. The Coxey Army, as it was called, would reach Washington, D.C., and march to the steps of the Capitol. After he and the marchers were beaten back by police, Coxey echoed the calls of the Chicago socialists in the decades before him: "Up these steps the lobbyists of trusts and corporations have passed unchallenged….We, the representatives of the toiling wealth-producers, have been denied."

Some have argued that this precedent of marching to the seat of national government has left open those mechanisms of democracy to serious threat, as happened on January 6, 2021. However, one must draw a clear distinction between the rightful use of citizen power and free speech in protests, be they for labor, immigration, civil rights or any other cause, versus the violent use of force to disrupt constitutional procedure and upend valid election results. More on that particular issue will come in a later chapter.

As the spring of 1894 began, strikes and lockouts were on the increase, and once again, Chicago found itself in the center of controversy. By April, committees of workers had tried unsuccessfully to negotiate with executives of the Pullman Company. On May 7, forty-one men and five women met with company executives regarding the pay cuts as well as the rents and utilities of the workers living in Pullmantown. The committee's suggestion of arbitration was denied by the company with the words that would be repeated throughout the summer, "There is nothing to arbitrate." The following day, several members of the committee were fired from the Pullman Company. The *Chicago Tribune*, in typical form, took up the position of the employer at this time. The editorials touted the negativity of strikes, that the Pullman Grievance Committee had done its job, unsuccessful though it turned out, that the members of the committee would have been let go in any event and that the company was operating at a loss. Chicago carpenter E.O. Cochran, an early leader of the Pullman movement, stated, "We will keep on trudging over the land knocking at the halls of legislation until the question of the unemployed is settled and wage slavery is driven out of the land….We demand work. We do not want soup."

Innovation was to govern much of the strike: the leadership would promote the notion of a living wage that would combine securing minimum pay and set a cap on hours worked, with the belief that more leisure time along with greater pay would mean more consumption by the working class. It was the classic "8 hours for work, 8 hours for rest, 8 hours for what we will" that was touted in the early 8-Hour Movement in the 1880s. However, the *Tribune* condemned this principle along with the newly founded American

Workers of the Pullman Palace Car Company on strike standing at the factory entrance in Pullmantown, May 1894. *Courtesy of the Newberry Library.*

Railway Union (ARU), headed by Eugene Victor Debs, as proselytizing to workers of Pullman. At the same time, the paper supported the owners of the railroads in their formation of the General Managers Association (GMA). The association was made up of the top managers of the twenty-four railroads based in or with lines that passed through Chicago. The companies represented had over $800 million in capital ($24.8 billion in 2021 purchasing power), controlled forty thousand miles of track and employed 221,000 men, women and children.

As the U.S. Strike Commission reported a year after the strike, "At least, so long as railroads are thus permitted to combine (in the G.M.A.) to fix wages and for their joint protection, it would be rank injustice to deny the right of all labor upon the railroads to unite for similar purpose."

Ironically, the spring elections in Chicago would be a harbinger for another sad tale in the city as well as the nation. As a growing number of Black citizens took their constitutional place in the electoral life of the community, many were "tripped up" by the Chicago political machine, an oft-repeated phrase describing the concretized, legitimized, corrupt, backroom governing body of the Second City in excluding certain citizens from seeking office.

An April 1894 editorial in the *Tribune* expressed "with great pain" that the "leading men of our colored race had approved of the independent running of a colored candidate for alderman in the 3rd Ward against the regular [read 'white'] nominee of the Republican Party…taken on the grounds of color." The hypocrisy of the attitude and the phrase is disturbing, albeit not surprising, in a city like Chicago where "on the grounds of color" has led to voter disenfranchisement; educational, housing and labor discrimination; not to mention race-based violence and profiling in the over one hundred years since the editorial was written.

Labor unions in general and the American Railway Union in particular had an opportunity at this point to ease some of the racial tensions in the nation but failed. Eugene Debs attempted the inclusion of the Pullman porters (exclusively Black workers in the company) in the union shortly after the founding of the ARU on June 21, 1893. In the delegate vote, after delivering an impassioned plea for unity of the working class, Debs's proposal at integration failed 112 to 110. Twenty years later, Chicago's most prominent Black-owned newspaper, *The Defender*, would repeat the warning against a divided labor front. The paper's founder, Robert Abbott, wrote in October 1915, "It seems strange that unions do not realize they will always have the black man as a competitor if he is shut out of their organization."

Eugene Debs (1908 photo), president of the American Railway Union and socialist candidate for the U.S. presidency in five of the six elections from 1900 to 1920, garnering 6 percent of the popular vote in 1912. *Courtesy of the Chicago History Museum (i009989_pm).*

It's important to note that the strike from May to late July 1894 ended unsuccessfully, even though hundreds of thousands of workers walked out directly or as sympathizers with the Pullman strikers. Labor's muscle would have flexed stronger, most probably successfully, with the force of the Pullman porters: a racially integrated and unified front could have led to the complete stoppage of the Pullman trains and likely the tie-up of the entire rail system in the country, forcing the hand of the government to insist on the company's arbitration and possibly bringing the GMA to heel through forced cooperation in bringing about a quick resolution.

Integration would have pushed the race issue with a positive force to the front of the public's attention and could have had the added benefit of showing the effectiveness of the unification of the working class against the elitist power and the encroaching arm of government at all levels that had continued to bed itself with the monied class. The fragmented socialist parties and traditionalist labor unions hold a major portion of responsibility for the failure of this particular strike.

Instead, the segregated union mounted a strong work stoppage by the end of June and effected a national supply chain crisis that necessitated eventual government intervention; however, as the strike continued into the Fourth of July holiday, pressure to find a resolution grew. Initially, George Pullman received major criticism for his intractable position of no arbitration with the union; the striking workers saw the decline of popular support for their efforts as violence erupted in Chicago from the first through the third of July and goods and services became noticeably scarcer. However, because the American Federation of Labor was unwilling to join the strike directly, the segregation of the ARU and the increased violence in Chicago and other cities, the efforts were destined to fail.

The immediate death blow to the strike came from the federal government just days before a call for a general national strike would likely have been issued: troops were called into the south side to quell the violence and stop track and roadhouse vandalism at the same time railroad lawyers and U.S. marshals' deputies joined forces against the strikers. The Strike Commission continued in its 1895 report:

> *3,600* [U.S. deputy marshals] *were selected by and appointed at the request of the General Managers Association, and of its railroads. They were armed and paid for by the railroads, and acted in the double capacity of railroad employees and U.S. officers.... This is placing officers of the government under the control of a combination of railroads. It is a bad precedent.*

The Sherman Anti-Trust Act of 1890 was invoked and upheld by the courts to deal with the American Railway Union, using a tool created to curb the power of monopolies in interstate commerce against the working class. The judgment fell against the strikers as an injunction was issued to ban "any combination that restrained trade among the states," including labor unions. Any action by a group of workers could be stopped, as industrialists were now free to cite interference of their free trade by any strikers. Once again, the strength of the powerholders was bolstered at the expense of the laborer. Debs and other union officials defended the strike by claiming that

A pregnant woman standing at the Chicago Stockyards, 1904. *Courtesy of the Chicago History Museum (DN-0000889_pm).*

the trains were not moving because of a lack of workers and not because of physical obstruction by the strike. The violence that had occurred in early July did not help this argument, but in essence, it was true: the intent of the strike was to cease work on the Pullman cars, not prohibit that work from being carried out in other areas.

Wielding his injunction, defended by the courts, President Grover Cleveland ordered federal troops to Illinois (over fourteen thousand and without any notification to Governor John Peter Altgeld, who protested the order), and on July 9 he issued a proclamation admonishing "all good citizens against aiding, countenancing, encouraging, or taking part in" any strike-related activity, even to the point of generalizing "unlawful obstructions, combinations, and assemblages" that would be interpreted as nefarious and that those who disregarded the warning would be seen as "public enemies." A striking worker was suddenly a criminal under the same category that the government would name John Dillinger and mafia bosses in the next century. Delegates of the strike, representing the Pullman workers, wired President Cleveland, denouncing corporations "drunk with the wine of special privilege," while pleading that he "no longer drink of the poisoned cup that is now being held to your lips."

JUDAS'S KISS

It was for naught. The army quelled most of the violence as Debs and several ARU executives were arrested for defying the injunction against the strike. According to Debs, "We will test the question as to whether men can be sent to jail without trial for organizing against capital." The verdict came down in the affirmative; Debs was sentenced to six months for conspiracy to interfere with interstate commerce. In 1895, the Supreme Court ruled in support of his conviction in the lower court, and he finished out the sentence at the McHenry County Jail in Woodstock, Illinois. It was Debs's belief that the ruling "left the law so biased that, in cases involving

Jane Addams and various aldermen with a crowd, July 22, 1915. *Courtesy of the Chicago History Museum. (DN-0064812).*

strikes at least, a man could be sent to prison without trial by jury" and that it made "every federal judge a Czar."

In the end, the damage to those directly affected by the strike was great. According to the Strike Commission, the total property destroyed was $685,000 ($21 million in 2021); the loss of railroad earnings was over $4.5 million ($140 million in 2021); the wages lost by the Pullman workers was $350,000 ($11 million in 2021); and the wages lost by all workers across the country was about $1.5 million ($46.5 million in 2021).

Even though the Pullman Strike of 1894 didn't reach the level of nationwide violence of the 1877 crisis, it did go further in showing the growing rift between the propertied class and the worker population. Jane Addams recounted in her *Twenty Years at Hull-House*, "During those dark days…the growth of class bitterness was most obvious." It would continue to be strained in the following decade with even more industrial strikes, though in the midst of this shadow came a stronger community effort to lead politicians in addressing important labor and civic issues in the poorer sections of the city.

Urged to Do Their Duty

Addams and residents of Hull-House pushed for enactment of state legislation that would protect young children from the "sweating system," the network of garment shops and factories where the largely female population (from eight years old on up) were subject to long hours, cramped work facilities and unhealthy conditions. Those who held little legislative power showed themselves to be the ones with the most creative solutions, if only they were to get a hearing. By 1889, Addams had observed city officials who were "public authorities never taking initiative and always waiting to be urged to do their duty." In the decade that encompassed the Pullman Strike and ended with the turn of the century, she struggled to achieve social change. Her words and actions would be echoed and reenforced by Ida B. Wells-Barnett in the next century.

In Addams's quarter-century memoir of Hull-House, she mourned a period of propaganda against constructive social effort:

> [It was] *the moment for marching and carrying banners, for stating general principles and making a demonstration, rather than the time for uncovering the situation and for providing the legal measures and the civic organization*

through which new social hopes might make themselves felt….I saw nowhere a more devoted effort to understand and relieve the heavy pressure [of urban life] *than the socialists were making, and I should have been glad to have had the comradeship of that gallant company had they not firmly insisted that fellowship depends upon identity of creed.*

She saw clearly a society that had split itself into camps based on emotion and passions rather than reason and principled thought directed at alleviating the specific woes of life in industrialized Chicago. The deadliest groups squaring off against each other were radicals working for complete social reorganization and those social fossils who "worshiped the god of things as they are," as Addams said, with no positions in the middle and with no efforts at concrete social improvements. The laws that were initially passed in 1892 to protect seamstresses in the Chicago sweatshops and limit their hours of work were struck down by the state supreme court as unconstitutional restraints on business. The new century would begin in the same manner that the old one had closed: labor unrest in Chicago's industrial neighborhoods rose as business interests and civic authority responded predictably with efforts to suppress them.

Industrial strikes continued and were fueled by women in the workplace with garment walkouts in 1905, 1910 and 1914 among the largest in Chicago. The force of Wells-Barnett and Addams was supplemented by the leadership of journalist Josephine Conger-Kaneko and her efforts in the suffrage movement. Illinois women received the vote in 1914, ahead of the Nineteenth Amendment's ratification in 1920. Conger-Kaneko had been the leading mouthpiece for the advancement of socialist candidates in Chicago's municipal elections since the turn of the century. She ran for city council in 1914, supporting other socialists (men and women) in several elections in which the capitalist parties of the city's political machine refused to support female candidates or advance real social change.

The resurrection of the once-prominent Socialistic Labor Party had morphed somewhat into the Industrial Workers of the World (IWW) in 1905 and held sway in more radical circles of the growing labor movement throughout the country. They would also receive the brunt of federal and municipal suspicion and ire during the First World War, as officials invoked clauses of the 1798 Alien and Sedition Act, the 1917 Espionage Act and the 1918 Sedition Act, which would become precursors to the twenty-first century's Patriot Acts of the G.W. Bush, Obama, Trump and Biden administrations.

Garment workers strike, 1910. *Courtesy of the Chicago History Museum (DN-0056132_pm).*

Mrs. Peter Farrell casting her ballot in Chicago, 1914. *Courtesy of the Chicago History Museum (DN-0062519_pm).*

Woman at a protest march against violence, September 2000. *Courtesy of Antonio Perez.*

After the Russian Revolution of 1917 and the victory of the "Reds," Soviet sympathizers and communists of any style of hammer and sickle in Chicago were routinely watched, arrested and deported. Eugene Debs ran for the presidency on the Socialist ticket in 1900, 1904, 1908 and 1912 (when he garnered over 900,000 votes, 6 percent of the total). In 1916, he ran unsuccessfully for the Indiana state legislature, and in 1920, he ran a fifth time as the Socialist nominee for the presidency. This time he was in prison, having been arrested in 1918 for protesting American involvement in the War to End All Wars.

By the time of the Great Depression, labor unrest was a predictable reality. National strikes in steel production, mining, the automotive industries and related fields reached crippling levels by 1934, with over 700,000 workers walking off their jobs in steel manufacturing alone that year. In his book *The 1937 Chicago Steel Strike,* John F. Hogan chronicles the escalation of violence that began in 1933 with the report of the then almost decadelong purchasing history of some of the steel manufacturers: they bought tear gas, up to four times the levels of any law enforcement agency in the country. A U.S. Senate subcommittee studying labor relations in the steel industry after the 1937 strikes noted, "The principal purpose of such weapons is aggression against unions... and hampers peaceful settlement of industrial disputes....Their use invites retaliatory violence."

In spite of seemingly reaching accords with various branches of a newborn and somewhat united but still racially segregated organized labor, the steel companies in Chicago were preparing for a face-off. Numerous walkouts and sit-downs (occupation of factories by workers) sprang up throughout the city in early 1937, and by May 26, tensions were once again strained to the point of crisis at the Republic Steel plant on the south side at 118th Street and Burley Avenue. And once again, city officials alongside law enforcement seemed to choose sides—assuming those with whom they bedded would be the safest route to peaceful resolution. And again, the fathers of the city were wrong.

When violence broke out on the thirtieth, Memorial Day weekend, striking workers were handily defeated, brutally beaten along with their family members and other bystanders with, according to the senate investigators, "axe-handle clubs and tear gas (used by police) that could have only come from Republic Steel." In the further investigation of the incident, it was clear that police officials and patrolmen had been in constant contact with company officials in the Republic plant, even to the point of being fed meals regularly at the company's expense, in the days leading up to the violence. At the same time, the company refused to negotiate with the committee of striking workers that sought the redress of their issues. Labor's voice remained in this weakened state because of the disunified, race-based distinction of the affected unions.

The choice of law and order over actual dialogue has plagued civil authority around the world. It's part of the nature of the beast Humanity to react with force when threatened. What is particularly frustrating is the willful stubbornness in Chicago that this tactic is the go-to choice time and time again. As has been stated throughout this book, creative solutions are needed to solve complex problems. And too often politicians in office ignore pleas for deeper thought and analysis of issues in order to find constructive solutions that are mutually beneficial to all involved. But the problem does not lie simply in our elected officials. We, the people, the voters, the citizens, the silent majority, bear a good amount of responsibility for the repetitious devolution into chaos in which we continually find ourselves being led. The public all too often demands quick fixes to problems and heckles any attempt at promoting long-term solutions. And the long-range solution is not simply civic involvement of the people. Better government comes with better citizens, indeed, but the quality of the governing also rises when the quantity of the governed who have a voice rises.

Enfranchisement of all citizens is key and has become one of the most critical points in modern politics. It was the greatest contest of will in the arena of American politics of the twentieth century—with nothing to compare it to but, as stated previously, the major concessions in the ancient world of the Romans opening the door to citizenship to non-Roman Italians of the entire peninsula 2,200 years ago. The need to erase as many distinctions of *we* and *they* is essential to greater social harmony.

What the ancient Italian tribes didn't have to face, with which a particular group of disenfranchised Americans did have to contend, was the denial of their own full humanity for 250 years based solely on skin color. After the recognition of the entire human being as a citizen who had been formerly enslaved, voting rights by law came to males over twenty-one (and all adults twenty-one and older in 1920 and eighteen and older in 1971). But the

Mexican immigrants awaiting deportation from Chicago, September 9, 1954. *Courtesy of the Chicago History Museum (DN-Q-5427).*

downside of the Thirteenth, Fourteenth and Fifteenth Amendments was the de facto condition that the newly enfranchised African Americans not attempt to exercise that right too much in particular areas of the country.

True enfranchisement would come with marches, blood, valor on the battlefield (abroad and at home), thought-filled argument and sheer strength of will. Social change and the rejection of ignorance, prejudice and any "ism" that we can belch out will come at a snail's pace, as the saying goes. But the snail does move forward, eventually, and does get to its destination.

6
RACE AGAINST TIME...TIME AND TIME AGAIN!

From Florida's stormy banks I'll go, I'll bid the South goodbye;
No longer will they treat me so. And knock me in the eye,
Hasten on my dark brother, Duck the Jim Crow law.
No Crackers North to slap your mother, or knock you on the jaw.
No Cracker there to seduce your sister, nor to hang you to a limb.
And you're not obliged to call 'em "Mister," nor skin 'em back at him.

—M. Ward, "Bound for the Promised Land," 1916

MORE THAN ENOUGH OPPORTUNITY

With the rise of that first generation of freed Americans from the chattel slave system beginning with Fredrick Douglass and Booker T. Washington, old enough to remember enslavement, more leaders and intellectuals like Ida B. Wells-Barnett and Robert Sengstacke Abbott came quickly along the path that they blazed. They all crossed paths along with thousands of others at the 1893 World's Fair in Chicago. Wells-Barnett had already established herself as an investigative journalist in Tennessee and would soon rise to leadership in the growing Black community in the Windy City that had just received the nickname; Abbott would find his voice through the most influential Black-owned newspaper in Chicago and the nation as a whole.

Racial issues had been left to fester within the entire country, the boil never having been fully lanced in the aftermath of war and Reconstruction or through legislation. Tensions rose with the growing numbers in Chicago of citizens freed from slavery along with their descendants joining the increasing immigrant population from southern and eastern Europe beginning around 1900. Wells-Barnett, like Jane Addams, was another citizen who would lead politicians from below and tried to effect social change, sometimes in spite of these same elected officials. Armed with education, a keen sense of issues and a courageous drive, she would move to the forefront of the early twentieth-century civil rights movement.

Ida B. Wells-Barnett, 1930. *Courtesy of the Chicago History Museum (i012868).*

Wells-Barnett, a Mississippian by birth, born into slavery by law in 1862, rose to notoriety in Memphis, Tennessee, as a thirty-year-old journalist exposing the lynchings of three of her friends by seventy-five hooded, white-robed men. One of her earliest salvos against this state-sponsored terrorism came in the aftermath: "Then these lynchers went quietly away and the bodies of the woman and three men were taken out and buried with as little ceremony as men would bury hogs." The offices at her newspaper, *Free Press*, were destroyed soon after this while she was in Philadelphia.

She would remain in the North through the next year, witness the greatness of the Chicago World's Fair in 1893, write for Black-owned newspapers in New York and Chicago and become the loudest clarion bell for the anti-lynching movement in the North and South for the next generation. Befriending Fredrick Douglass and the *Chicago Defender* owner/editor Robert Abbott, she was energized to take on the campaign that would lead her to investigative efforts into the post–World War I violence against Black homeowners. But her warnings of major strife on the horizon before the summer of 1919 were ignored by Chicago's power-wielders.

Wells-Barnett, in one of her first Chicago-based efforts to expose lynching, traveled to Cairo, Illinois, in 1909 after the murder of Will James, a Black man accused of killing a white girl. Mob justice dictated that there be no trial, and he was taken from his jail cell. In the presence of the sheriff and thousands of onlookers, he was hanged, shot enough times that the rope around his neck was torn away from the scaffold and his corpse burned. Through her work, Wells-Barnett pressured Governor Charles Samuel Deneen to oust the Alexander County sheriff. Robert Abbott wrote of her, "If we only had a few men with the backbone of Mrs. Barnett, lynching would soon come to a halt in America." Sexist though the sentiment may seem to the twenty-first-century reader, Ida B. Wells-Barnett rose to prominence of her own accord and would remain a leader in her own right for the rest of her life.

Tensions based on skin color escalated between Americans in the first fifteen years of the new century. Robert Abbott rose to prominence with his establishment in Chicago of *The Defender* in 1905; the paper became a leading voice of journalism across the country for over seventy-five years. Beginning with the rewriting of stories from conventional newspapers into stories from an African American perspective, Abbott was able to raise the level of what would be considered a truer objectivity and fact-finding. His breakthrough work involved the continued exposition, along with Wells-Barnett, of rampant lynching and shameless ignoring of three constitutional amendments that governed freedom and equality of citizenship continuing in the South and parts of the North.

The newspaper "went viral" in those early days, due in large part to Abbott's recruitment of the Pullman porters, workers on the transcontinental passenger train. The porters brought him the discarded newspapers of major cities that white passengers left behind. He and his staff would rewrite the major stories and expand on them. In the same way, porters were solicited to deliver stacks of the weekly to newsstands and other hubs in cities where the trains stopped, and in a matter of a few years, the *Chicago Defender* was as well known in some circles as the *New York Times* and the *Chicago Tribune*. Abbott was the editor of the first Black-owned paper with a dedicated sports page and is credited with the earliest efforts for the desegregation of sports in particular and racial equity in general. The paper was instrumental in publicizing the issues of the 1914 porter negotiations with the Pullman Company, though the talks were unsuccessful for the workers.

When the 1915 silent film *Birth of a Nation* was released and due to arrive in Chicago, Abbott and others (including Mayor "Big Bill" Thompson) led protests against it. Ethan Michaeli, in his history of *The Defender*, notes the reconstitution of the formerly defunct Ku Klux Klan after the film was made in the rituals, specifically cross burnings, and the policies of the KKK, which rose in popularity. In spite of a 111–2 vote in the Illinois legislature to prohibit any art that "tends to incite race riot or race hatred," the ban was lifted by court order, and *Birth of a Nation* premiered in Chicago on June 5.

Theater critic Kitty Kelly waxed racially in her positive review of the film: "We must have villains of some sort, and if every nationality becomes so sensitive, soon we will have none but American villains." And again, the we/ they dichotomy is taken as legitimate.

It needs to be noted that this author has watched the nearly three-and-a-half-hour uncut version that shows the main villains to be a "mulatto" ex-slave who becomes lieutenant governor of South Carolina and a group of former slaves in the South Carolina state legislature who do nothing but eat, drink, carouse and sleep with their feet on the desks during legislative sessions. The Klan members are shown as victims of an unjust postwar world, robbed of their happy slaves who were content to remain in servitude, and the former enslavers are shown struggling to regain their dignity. At the end of the film, the hooded heroes literally ride to the rescue of the poor former enslavers as they are being besieged by crazed Black men.

At the time that *Birth of a Nation* debuted, *The Defender* and Wells-Barnett were continuing to expose southern racist practices as the brutality of lynchings increased. Fueling the Great Migration in its earliest pre–World War I days, Abbott wrote: "If you can freeze to death in the North and be free, why freeze to death in the south and be a slave? *The Defender* says come." With the First World War in full force, immigration from Europe decreased considerably and the "Second Emancipation," the "Second Exodus," was in full swing, from South to North, thanks in large part to the newspaper. Wells-Barnett stepped up her attacks on lynchings and became the most virulent scourge to the stagnant moral supremacy of the white South and its defenders in Washington, D.C., who refused to push for the federal criminalization of lynching by fact, not simply by platitude.

Chicago author Carl Sandburg contributed opinion pieces to the paper. He reflected on the phenomenon of the Great Migration in 1919:

> *Not only is Chicago a receiving station and port of refuge for colored people who are anxious to be free from the jurisdiction of Lynch Law, but there has been built here a publicity or propaganda machine that directs its appeals or carries on an agitation that each week reaches hundreds of thousands of the colored race in the southern states.*

The rise of the Klan in those first decades of the century elicited a fresh sense of city unity in 1921. After a heavy recruitment effort by the KKK in Chicago and throughout Illinois, clergy and business owners in the city rallied against them after a *Tribune* editorial commended the Klan. Religious leaders of many denominations and businessmen throughout the city, members of the American Unity League, printed the names of 150 Chicago Klansmen and distributed the leaflets throughout the city. The shaming accomplished its task, as the exposed lost business and public respect, and new membership in the Klan dropped significantly. *The Defender* kept up its attacks throughout the decade, culminating in a 1928 front-page challenge titled "Who Won the Rebel War?"

> *Today the South reigns supreme in its own code of injustice. Actual slavery has given way to peonage: prison camps and mine prisons. Disenfranchisement still plays its part. Segregation, discrimination on the basis of color, still plays its flagrant role in the workings of our government. Sixty-five years after the war of rebellion, thirty years after the Spanish-American War and ten years after the war for the sublime doctrine of world equality, and the rebel flag still waves over America, still waves its dirty bars over the Stars and Stripes, which symbolize the independence of man!*

In the midst of the shaming of the South through exposé, the North showed itself as hardly the Promised Land for the now second and third generations of freed human beings trying to share the blessings of liberty. The summer of 1917 saw racial tensions explode in East St. Louis, Illinois, which should have served as more than enough warning of things to come. The *Tribune* saw it but focused, as was its habit, on the wrong area. In an article titled "Half a Million Darkies," a reporter stated that "the negro *problem* [emphasis added] has moved north with a vengeance, and the North does not yet begin to realize it—even with the outrage at East St. Louis still sounding its terrible warning."

The emphasized word, *problem*, expresses the whole lopsided issue of the past three centuries of chattel slavery and the apartheid that followed. A problem needs a solution. One problem, one solution. When one group is the problem, another group needs to provide the solution. Again, Antonio Gramsci offers some insight. He inherited a limping Socialist Party that refused to lead the working class into a post–World War I socially revolutionized Italy that would have included the northern industrial proletariat alongside the southern and Sicilian/Sardinian rural farmers. He recast "The Southern Problem," as it was known, into "The Southern Question" and posed other pertinent questions in relation to the Italian nation as a whole.

In the United States, following the Civil War, the question of slavery was assumed to have been answered—the problem was supposed to have been solved with freedom. But all the pertinent issues surrounding 250 years of race-based servitude, the subsequent debates regarding racial equality, the reality of free labor suddenly gone, were left in relative abandon after the eleven years of northern occupation of the South had been prematurely terminated. The question was hardly addressed, let alone solved.

A WAR TO END ALL WAR?
NEITHER "OVER THERE" NOR OVER HERE

The American involvement in the First World War from 1917 through the Treaty of Versailles in 1919 provided the impetus to force the confrontation of the issues of segregation and racial inequity back home. The experiences of Black soldiers in French cities and on the battlefield, under an integrated command of Black officers alongside their French counterparts, revealed a different reality than the vast majority of these Americans had ever experienced in the United States. In interviews after the war, *The Defender* exposed the transplanting of segregation in Europe only by white soldiers and commanders of the American army; no one else seemed to see color as a defining attribute.

The French commander of the 370th Regiment of the American Expeditionary Force (the U.S. Army's 8th Regiment), composed primarily of Black American soldiers, said in his final orders, as reported by *The Defender* in its February 22, 1919 issue: "The blood of your comrades who fell on the soil of France mixed with the blood of our soldiers, renders indissoluble the bonds of affection that unite us."

Chicagoans of the 8th Regiment received a rousing welcome home from the Great War. And thanks in part to Abbott's marketing efforts, a racially integrated celebration was organized when the regiment returned. Brigadier General Franklin Denison was particularly honored, having reached the highest rank of an African American soldier at that time. Others were upheld with awards from both France and the United States: sixty-eight men received the French honor of the Croix de Guerre; twenty-one received the American award, the Distinguished Service Cross (fewer than one-third of those same soldiers recognized by the French), with one soldier having been awarded the Distinguished Service Medal. The regiment suffered a 20 percent casualty rate, with ninety-five killed and over five hundred wounded.

American soldiers as a whole set themselves apart in service to the effort and suffered the physical and emotional trauma that all wars bring. While the causes of that war are seen less romantically today, the reasons for American involvement at the time were touted as a grand enterprise to defend democracy and end war and tyranny forever. The ugly reality set in after the parades were swept away. Once the Black soldiers who fought for liberty, equality and fraternity in France settled back on the homefront, they had to slide back down the social ladder of the Land of the Free and Home of the Brave.

Housing segregation and its accompanying acts of terror served as a massive pile of kindling in the several months before major rioting was to break out in the summer of 1919. Wells-Barnett branched into this area of investigation and offered words of warning to city officials. After the violence in East St. Louis two years earlier, she was a consistent voice of admonition to a city government in Chicago slow to enforce laws related to the victimization of Black homeowners trying to move freely throughout the city—a reality that would plague the city for decades afterward. The pattern followed the violence of the South; bombings of Black citizens' homes, churches and businesses rose after 1915.

The sometimes unspoken but oftentimes acted on racism seethes when "they" begin to rise to a level equal to "us." In the essay "Inheritance" in *The 1619 Project*, Trymaine Lee identifies this point as one of the most pervasive and destructive effects of racism—the inability of Black families in the United States to acquire wealth in any form, unlike white families. Taking into account the generational prohibition against slaves owning property until the late nineteenth century; the denial of reparations after emancipation; the enactment of apartheid legislation dictating segregation in schools, businesses, marriage and other social networking in the North and South; as well as the lack of confidence of citizens of color to equal protection by civil authorities that has extended well into the twenty-first century, it is not surprising that there is a wealth gap along the color line. And the chasm only widens when one takes into account the acts of violence to which Black families have been subjected for a century after the Civil War.

By 1919, Wells-Barnett had become a consistent voice in the ears of city officials, taking them to task for their inaction in the face of a growing number of acts of racial violence against Black citizens, homeowners and business owners. With the work of *The Defender* and Wells-Barnett, more attention was given to a series of house bombings that spring. Chicago real estate giant Jesse Binga, a former Pullman porter, and his family survived seven bombings of their home between 1919 and 1921. The bombs, typical of the terrorist tactics in the South and in Chicago, were never capable of total destruction: American racists are capitalists first and foremost and would never do anything to damage their own structures or bring down their own property values by detonating a more powerful device. After the last bombing of Binga's home on September 1, 1921, *The Defender* archived his declaration that it would not be repaired: "I will let my home stand as a monument to Chicago law and disorder." Mayor Thompson refused to see Wells-Barnett and her committee, which had been giving fair warning of imminent civil decay if the rot of racism were not addressed in the violence that had become too commonplace in those early months of 1919.

Justification of housing segregation takes on an even more ridiculous quality with unsubstantiated claims of economics: the always-to-be-worshiped god Private Property is given homage only when a particular group is talking about this divinity in relation to themselves. "We" have a right to "our" own property, but the fact that "they" wish to become owners of their own property is subject to "our" approval. And once the devotees of this brick-and-mortar front lawn ornament god get nervous enough, their methods of keeping the races separate become violent. Carl Sandburg interviewed L.M. Smith, one of the self-appointed high priests of this race-based, divinely bestowed territorialism. Smith was president of the Kenwood Improvement Association in 1919, and in the wake of the spring bombings, he said:

> *They* [Black homeowners] *injure our* [white homeowners'] *investments. They hurt our values. I couldn't say how many have moved in, but there's at least a hundred blocks* [that] *are tainted. We are not making any threats, but we do say that something must be done.*

Sandburg concluded that the reality of the property value argument was quite the opposite from Smith's and others' claims: according to his investigation, rents for Black tenants tended to be increased by $35–$50 per month ($500–$750 per month in 2021 purchasing power) compared to what white tenants were charged for equitable space and in similar neighborhoods. He reported, "The fact is that it wasn't an open market. It was a panicky market." These attitudes and practices, not unique to Chicago, were not unknown to city officials. While Mayor Thompson campaigned successfully for reelection in 1919, he won by the narrowest of margins of all his tenures as city chief. He recognized the importance of the votes of his Black constituents and was a strong supporter of racial equality in Chicago. However, change came at a glacial pace in spite of Thompson's intentions and the efforts of Wells-Barnett and Abbott to keep attention on the inequity and violence that fell disproportionately on the city's Black population.

In 1919, race-fired violence exploded across the country during what would be identified as the Red Summer. The level of bloodshed, the speed with which the hatred ignited and its transcontinental sweep demonstrate that, as usual, an individual incident did not cause the conflagration. A single incident lit a match that set the whole stack of fire-ready kindling ablaze: on Sunday, July 27, Eugene Williams was struck on the head by a rock thrown by a white man and drowned while floating near the 29th Street beach with friends, having unintentionally drifted into the "whites only" part of Lake Michigan (an apparent oversight of the creator of the universe that left it to human beings to segregate the water and sand). From this, Chicago and the nation exploded in several days of violence.

City officials struggled with which power move to put into place, giving themselves the typical choices of the creatively deprived: the options were limited to the deployment of a majority of the Chicago police force or calling up the Illinois National Guard in addition to declaring martial law. Politics dictated policy as the mayor dared not be seen as needing outside help, so the police were called on to act, ill-prepared and some unwilling, in the defense of the besieged Black population.

The surroundings near 31st Street and Lake Michigan and the memorial to Eugene Williams and all the victims of 1919's "Red Summer." *Courtesy of Nathanael Filbert.*

At the same time, neighborhood gangs powered up their presence on the south side. Young men of the white neighborhoods, many of them descendants of those early refugees from famine-ridden Ireland seventy-five years earlier, sought to secure their patrimony by terrorizing others, with tactics by which even their ancestors had not been brutalized. Members of Regan's Colts and the Hamburgers (to which a seventeen-year-old future mayor Richard J. Daly belonged), with the complicity or closed eyes of the police, engaged in intimidation tactics—terrorizing individuals as well as groups and destroying private property—that would be copied, observed Gary Krist in his *City of Scoundrels*, less than fifteen years later in Nazi Germany.

With no options remaining, the mayor and governor decided to call up the National Guard, and order was restored after a full week of chaos. In the end, the statistics were clear: 38 deaths had been recorded in the city, with 23 Black and 15 white citizens losing their lives; 537 injured, with the racial division of two-thirds to one-third, respectively; and between 1,000 and 2,000 left homeless, mostly Black home or business owners and tenants. The numbers don't include, nor can they record, the rise in tensions in the aftermath, the further wedge driven between Black citizens and the Chicago Police Department (similar to the ill-will and suspicions the Germans held against the police in the last half of the nineteenth century) and the loss of credibility of elected officials in the eyes of all voters regardless of race.

Some flawed histories record the events of the 1919 race riots as if they were merely a nationwide uprising of Black Americans fed up with injustice and mistreatment. While the riots were on one hand a race-based groaning for equality fifty years after the end of slavery, there was also an even bigger reaction against such action: the targets of violence and destruction were primarily along the color line, the victims primarily Black. There were no roving gangs of Black citizens terrorizing white citizens; white workers were not pounced on as they left the stockyards at the end of their shifts; and the police department would not have allowed bands of Black youth to carry out vigilante justice. These actions by white gangs and citizens against members of the African American community were witnessed and recorded.

Mayor Thompson, castigated for his inaction in the wake of the spring home bombings and even more so after the summer riots, was defeated in his 1923 attempt at reelection, only to rise again in 1927. It's a tragic staple of the Chicago political machine that lubricates its revolving door, allowing for incompetents and the criminally negligent to easily return to city hall.

Wells-Barnett was active from the beginning of the violence. Condemning the city's inaction (and in some cases the police's blatant aiding and abetting

The inscription on the 1919 memorial stone, dedicated in 2009 by the students of York High School in Elmhurst, Illinois. *Courtesy of Nathanael Filbert.*

the rioters), she wrote, "Lawless mobs roam our streets. They kill inoffensive citizens and no notice is taken. They are Negroes—they are only Negroes— and it doesn't matter." The day after the murder of Eugene Williams, she began interviewing witnesses and victims in preparation for the investigations for which she planned to push after peace was to be restored. By day 3 of the violence, she was calling for the creation of a biracial committee for just such a purpose. The *Chicago Daily Journal* published her statement on the front page that day, in its entirety. She set her sights on those elected officials who played the political game and were getting burned in the flames of the riots as her statement continued: "Chicago is weak and helpless before the mob. Notwithstanding our boasted democracy, lynch law is king."

The Chicago Commission on Race Relations, the brainchild of Wells-Barnett, came out with a six-hundred-page report, *The Negro in Chicago: A Study of Race Relations and a Race Riot*, in 1922, both as an archive of the events in Chicago and the entire state during that summer of 1919 as well as a detailed look at causality that went beyond the specific events of that violent week. The work is broken down into segments that address the migration of

Black citizens from South to North, the Black population in Chicago itself, housing and employment issues, the levels of contact between the races, crime and public opinion. There are recommendations to law enforcement, elected officials, educators and parks officials, civic organizations, labor unions, churches and social agencies, as well as every citizen despite skin color. The hope was to make the necessary changes begin at every level of government and of society, slow to come as they might be.

The details of the violence are well presented in Michaeli's history of *The Defender* and in Krist's *City of Scoundrels*. Again, this work's intent is to highlight the causes, as well as the "What could have been done differently?" of the event. Sadly, as if on constant repeat, the city's actions bear out depressingly the incompetence, neglect, maliciousness and intransigence of its alleged leaders. A mix of citizens presented a quilting of solutions and policies that had been consistently ignored by the powerful elected to lead—who should have had the humility and wisdom to follow others when those others were doing the actual leading.

Concrete efforts made often crumble against the brick wall of bureaucracy and human intransigence. And this is what happened in the wake of the 1922 commission report. City officials, businessmen and real estate moguls, all members of the propertied class, saw the solution quite differently from the investigators: racial harmony was an impossibility, therefore people must be kept separate. LaDale Winling, in a meticulous study of decades of Cook County's housing records, uncovered the city's ugly reality through what are called restrictive covenants: "No part of said premises shall be sold, given, conveyed, or leased to any negro or negroes." The covenants were also used to restrict the movement of the Jewish population and any others of "them" in Chicago. The work of Winling's team has been collected and digitized in the Newberry Library.

With the 1896 *Plessy v. Ferguson* case codifying the separate-but-equal lie of most aspects of American life, restrictive covenants in many parts of the country became the norm in less than twenty years after the court's ruling. More protests against inequitable and segregated housing followed through the next three decades in Chicago. White riots erupted again on the south side in 1943 and into the 1960s, most notoriously during Dr. Martin Luther King's 1965 Chicago Freedom March. The Bridgeport neighborhood, home of reigning mayor Richard J. Daley, became the scene of violence against the marchers, including King himself.

By 1937, *The Defender* had become the city's mouthpiece against restrictive covenants, launching a publicity campaign that made race-based restrictions more difficult to defend, as the world was beginning to hear the first inklings of Nazi racial theory playing out against Germany's Jewish population: "If one covenant in any city is legal, every covenant may become legal and a whole city, a whole county, or even a whole state may become so restricted that our Race may be forbidden to live anywhere within its borders." In two years, the paper would make the plea again, focusing on an appeal to Chicago's Polish population in the wake of the 1939 German-Soviet invasion of Poland.

In spite of the worldwide effort to stop fascist aggression overseas, more acts of violence were perpetrated against Black homeowners daring to cross the color line and live wherever they wished in the United States. This included real estate investor Carl Hansberry and his family. According to Winling, Carl's daughter and future author Lorraine Hansberry was "berated and harassed" on her way to school near 61ˢᵗ Street, which ended up feeding her passion that erupted in her 1959 play, *A Raisin in the Sun*. It was the Supreme Court's *Hansberry v. Lee* case of 1940, unsuccessful though it was in declaring restrictive covenants unconstitutional, that paved the way eight years later in *Shelley v. Kraemer* for the declaration of the covenants' unenforceability based on the equal protection clause of the Fourteenth Amendment.

Even without the issue of racial segregation, city officials struggled to find solutions to the housing issues. By the beginning of the twentieth century, the mostly Sicilian poor of the near north side had settled in what would become known as Little Hell. By 1915, extortionists of the Mafia (genially referred to as the "Black Hand") had begun to hold residents hostage to their urban terrorist tactics. Between the world wars, crime went almost unchecked, as the police and city officials ignored some of the crime (for which they were rewarded handsomely) and other acts of violence, for which they received little help from victims or anyone in the neighborhood because of the same fear-based code of silence that hampers legitimate law enforcement to this day (a downside of the constitutional right to face one's accuser!). Lawrence J. Vale, in his *Purging the Poorest: Public Housing and the Design Politics of Twice-Cleared Communities*, notes that before the Depression more than one-third of the murders in the city were committed in Little Hell, where the Sicilians accounted for only 5 percent of Chicago's population.

The neighborhood would change only in name and racial makeup after the Second World War: the Cabrini-Green Housing Project rose (and fell) on the smoldering spot of its predecessor, with city officials convinced that bulldozers and architects could solve the ongoing issues of economic disparity and racial inequality.

The 1956 Bud Billiken Parade, an ongoing annual celebration of African American life since 1929 on the city's south side, featured Harry S Truman, John Sengstacke (nephew of *Chicago Defender* founder Robert Sengstacke Abbott) and Mayor Richard J. Daley. *Courtesy of the Chicago Urban League.*

Before the enforcement of basic housing rights as well as the partial overturning of *Plessy* in 1954 with *Brown v. The Board of Education of Topeka, Kansas*, the federal government hampered efforts at housing equity through the Franklin Roosevelt administration's Home Owners' Loan Corporation and the Federal Housing Administration of the 1930s and 1940s. Agents traveled the country in an attempt to stabilize the housing market in the midst of the Great Depression, assuming the government was more than capable of solving the economic problems from the top down.

In his unique study of urban renewal and gentrification, Daniel Kay Hertz writes in *The Battle of Lincoln Park* that in an ill-conceived plan of purchasing home mortgages from banks, the government actually solidified housing segregation and disinvestment in poorer (read: primarily Black and Brown) neighborhoods across the country. Redlining was the practice of these agents looking at city maps and highlighting in green those neighborhoods where federal support would be forthcoming and in red those areas deemed "hazardous" for investment and therefore ineligible for federal money. It was truly a metaphorical death sentence for many neighborhoods across the country, as well as a literal one for generations of Black and Brown youth.

The Chicago neighborhoods designated as undesirable for investment spiraled into years of blight and would be sacrificed further beginning in the 1950s as plans were drawn up to amputate huge swaths of homes (according to Hertz, up to forty thousand homes between 1948 and 1958, housing hundreds of thousands of individuals) for what would become the city's expressway nightmare—without any input from residents. Once again, elected officials, assuming omniscience, acted without regard for consequences. "We" know what is best, and "they" will do what "we" say. Neighborhoods of the poorer south and west sides of the city were severed as a convenient escape route was paved for further racial segregation into safe white suburbs. The expressways doubled as bridges of flight in addition to being walls that further segregated the city, and elected officials, complicit in this asphalt apartheid, would continue to wring their hands, fumbling for a way out of increased urban deterioration.

Narrow-minded politicians and self-serving developers have teamed up, according to Hertz, in the city's attempt to build a city for all. Their flaws seem deep-seated; their intentions may be remotely benign, but their methods have led to an urban malignancy that defies curing. The fatal paternalism had raised its hand again, just as city fathers did after the Great Fire, just as the defenders of law and order did after the labor upheavals of the late nineteenth century and just as elected officials did into the twentieth century. Krist highlights the father-knows-best attitude

Young men learning of apprenticeships in the construction industry at a Chicago Urban League–sponsored event in the Altgeld Gardens neighborhood in the 1950s. *Courtesy of the Chicago Urban League.*

of the post–Red Summer leadership of Mayor Thompson and others who would follow, tragically pertinent for all times as well:

Reform, for all its good intentions, too often puts the city's struggling masses in the role of children, wards of the state who had to be cared for and improved through the wise guidance of a privileged, well-educated native-born white elite. Thompsonism, for all its venality, actually gave them a measure of real representation in government.

And again and again, voters have been and still are either discouraged from voting for fresh voices or they buy into, election after election, the MachineSpeak of the politicians: the elected have the answers for everything, and their opponents don't. It's the same dribble that has leaked from the bilge faucets from city hall to the White House to Capitol Hill and back to sweet home Chicago. This Orwellian interpretation of reality would continue into the turbulence of the second half of the twentieth century and face off against a relatively united front of race, gender and orientation, hellbent on ending war, poverty and any "ism" that could be conjured.

7

CHICAGO STRUTTING

Black Power, Flower Power, Rainbows and Unicorns

Empire got too big, cities too crazy, garbage-filled Rome
full of drunken soldiers, fat politicians,
circus businessmen—
safer, healthier life on a farm, make yr own wine
in Italy, smoke yr own grass in America.
—Allen Ginsberg, *"Ecologue,"* The Fall of America, *1970*

TIRED OF BEING TIRED

On March 2, 1955, Claudette Colvin, fifteen years old and pregnant, refused to give up her seat next to white girls and move to the back of a bus in Montgomery, Alabama, nine months before Rosa Parks. Colvin was arrested for defying the state's segregation law and the city's ordinance for racial separation on public transportation, for disorderly conduct and for assaulting a police officer after she kicked one of them. She was named as one of the plaintiffs in the lawsuit that dismantled segregation in that city and, eventually, across the country.

On August 28, 1955, Chicagoan Emmett Till, fourteen years old, was kidnapped, tortured and lynched by a white mob in Drew, Mississippi, for allegedly "flirting or whistling" at a twenty-one-year-old white woman. His open casket in Chicago let the world "see what they did to my boy," in the words of his mother, Mamie Elizabeth Till-Mobley, adding fuel to another generation of activists.

On December 1, 1955, Rosa Parks, forty-two years old, defied the order of a bus driver in Montgomery, Alabama, to move from a row of seats in the "colored section" for a white passenger because the "white section" was full. Her arrest led to a yearlong boycott of the city's buses, launching the modern civil rights movement.

In the first fifty years of the twentieth century, the United States fought in two world wars, allegedly for freedom and democracy, for an end to imperialism and fascism, for all people to live in peace. The second half of that century witnessed more war, the constant threat of nuclear annihilation and the ever-present dichotomy in society of "we" and "they." And nowhere was this division more pronounced than in the ongoing racial struggle that had plagued the nation since the first African slaves were forced into the Western Hemisphere in the early part of the seventeenth century. The armed forces had been desegregated, and pressure was kept up on the Truman and Eisenhower administrations to lead more strongly by desegregating the federal levels of government. *The Defender* kept up its pressure as the new editor and nephew of founder Robert Abbott, John H. Sengstacke, took on major advisory roles in those postwar years in Washington.

Even as racial segregation was being challenged in the former Confederacy, tensions between black and white Chicagoans tightened. Integrated neighborhoods and schools became heated topics across the city, and as in the previous one hundred years, it became the task of citizens to lead the politicians down the path of solution. Empowered by a Supreme Court that seemed more ready than any previous set of justices to protect citizens' rights by destroying the final vestiges of the apartheid-dripping Jim Crow laws of both North and South, marches against housing discrimination, economic inequality and school segregation became more common. Peaceful activism, nonviolent civil disobedience and public outcries all became commonplace as the 1960s progressed, but still resistance to change solidified.

School desegregation became the flashpoint as the 1963 academic year was just about to start in Chicago. The obstinate superintendent of the Chicago Public Schools Benjamin Willis refused the high court's integration orders given nine years earlier. Mayor Richard J. Daley, in typical Chicago executive fashion, ignored the overwhelming support that the Black community (33 percent of the city's population at that time) had given him in that spring's election. Overcrowded classrooms in Black neighborhood schools were not addressed with any real effort. Willis's solution was to ignore the fact that school classrooms in white neighborhoods were underpopulated. Rather than mix the students, he first ordered Black students to be split in their hours

A protest march against education discrimination and segregation in Chicago, 1966. *Courtesy of the Chicago Urban League.*

in school—half of the student body of a given school would go during the early part of the day, and the other half would attend late in the day. That being a complete failure, he ordered the installation of mobile classrooms to absorb the overflow. These "Willis Wagons," as they were affectionately dubbed by protestors, were poorly ventilated, cramped and shabbily built.

By mid-August, organized protests had been set up around many of the schools' "wagons." The brutality of the police's suppression of the protestors that day was mirrored in photographs and eyewitness reports from *The Defender*. As clubs and boots were used to quell those arrested, pictures were published side by side, showing the Chicago officers in similar posture that their club and fire hose–wielding cohorts in Birmingham, Alabama, had been in before them against civil rights marchers, with the caption, "A short three months was all it took for police brutality to move north." Again, city officials sure of themselves and their own unmovable positions placed blame on a population long suffering from bureaucratic neglect, disenfranchisement and high-handed paternalism.

On October 22, a massive school boycott was launched, with almost 225,000 students skipping classes that day. Downtown protests centered on school board headquarters and were joined by up until then silent aldermen from the six predominantly Black wards. In February, a second boycott led to 172,000 students walking out. Mayor Daley and the Chicago Machine won out: Willis remained in office as school superintendent through the summer of 1966.

In spite of court orders in 1980 and 2009, there are still race-based inequalities in the Chicago Public School system. School closures in the south and west sides during the administration of Mayor Rahm Emanuel were weighted heavily against Black students, with eleven thousand displaced after fifty schools were closed in 2013. The promise to citizens that the school buildings would be sold and the spaces turned into community-beneficial structures had not materialized even five years after the abandonment. Again, the people of the city are misled, almost as naively as the hogs to the butcher in the old stockyards on the city's south side: promises are made that sound good, only to be revealed as the empty ramblings of politicians who seem to bide their time (every time) until the next election.

It is important to note that, while Chicago has suffered through appointed school boards and superintendents since 1872 at the whim and beck and call of mayors, the 150-year-old wall is cracking and is soon to come down: through state mandate, and in spite of Mayor Lori Lightfoot's opposition, the citizens of Chicago will elect all members and the superintendent of its first democratic school board by 2026.

Throughout the 1960s, in the aftermath of the Kennedy/King/Kennedy assassinations and the midst of the horrors of yet another war for democracy, civil unrest erupted in a continued stream as if the body politick were hemorrhaging. The assassination of Dr. Martin Luther King Jr. by Illinoian James Earl Ray on April 4, 1968, set off a series of protests and riots across the country as yet another Black person rising to a high level was knocked down—the last straw in a pile of parched kindling that had again been left untended. In spite of further efforts of those holding to the King philosophy of nonviolent resistance for social change, the time had come for many others who had patiently accepted peaceful protest in the previous generation to take more direct action. Black Power movements rose to spearhead more aggressive tactics that soon would be imitated by antiwar efforts, women's rights activists and the gay/lesbian self-outings by the end of the decade.

A more in-your-face orientation, not backing away from physical confrontations, and even the use of violence were all acceptable forms of protest and class action in addition to high-visibility community aid like free lunch programs for the political arm of the movement, the Black Panther Party. A new determination would be encapsulated in the 1968 Summer Olympics in Mexico City as Texan Tommie Smith and New Yorker John Carlos raised their fists during the medal awards ceremony, the iconic symbol of Black Power since the early '60s.

The murder of twenty-one-year-old Fred Hampton in Chicago on December 4, 1969, marks yet another milestone covered in blood. This founder of the Rainbow Coalition of young activists (some would say gang

A civil rights advocate gives the iconic "Black Power" salute as she marches in Chicago, 1966. *Courtesy of the Chicago Urban League.*

members) of the Black, white and Latin communities was part of the National Black Panther Party and an avowed communist, both constitutionally protected forms of political expression. With the wrath of Mayor Daley and the backing of a still-paranoid Federal Bureau of Investigation that saw "Reds" in every crack of the status quo, Hampton and twenty-two-year-old Mark Clark would suffer their outburst: after a shootout and deaths of two Chicago police officers and a Blank Panther member that previous November, the city decided to act against the leaders.

At about 4:00 a.m. on the fourth, heavily armed police officers broke into Hampton's home, shot Clark, who was guarding the entrance, and then went into the bedroom and shot a drugged Hampton (secobarbital having been put into his drink by a police plant) as he slept next to his partner, Akua Njeri, nine months pregnant with Fredrick Junior. An inquest that was convened afterward found the killings to be justifiable homicide, but a civil rights lawsuit soon followed. Eventually, the families of Clark and Hampton were awarded settlements from the city, Cook County and the federal government in 1982. Justice served, in a sense, a decade later still does not address the constant in Chicago's dealing with civil unrest and against strong leaders who defy the status quo.

Into contemporary times, the pattern is tragic in its predictability. With the nationwide unrest caused by the high-profile 1991 beating of Rodney King in Los Angeles, there seems to be a much lower threshold of quiet acceptance of the racial biases of law enforcement. Closer to our own period in Chicago, from the killing of Laquan McDonald in 2014 by Officer Jason Van Dyke, to the 2021 deaths (almost simultaneously) of Adam Toledo and Anthony Alvarez, to the crippling injuries into the death of a thirteen-year-old boy (unnamed because of his age) in mid-2022 by "Officer John Doe" and especially after the murder of Anton Black in 2018 and the 2020 killings of Breonna Taylor and George Floyd, people have begun to rise up in relative unison to end the nationwide shoot-to-kill orders that seem to have been disseminated to officers on the ground in many American cities.

The stress and tensions of the lives of police officers notwithstanding, we as a society have got to look at civil order differently. Rather than taking our model of law and order from a militaristic mold, politicians would be well advised to deal with the abject poverty of the crime-ridden neighborhoods that breed poverty's pestilence; the untreated mental illness and drug addictions of fellow citizens, off of which crime often feeds; and the disinvestment in these areas of the city that suffer from the very things that cause businesses and political bosses to cower in fear of touching the poorer neighborhoods.

And again, in exchange for our politicians' inability to act, for their always-at-the-ready high-handed condemnations of crime and gang activity, we the people reward them again and again and again with reelection. With few exceptions such as the minor shake-up of the Chicago City Hall in 2019 with several incumbent city council members losing their seats, and with the success of six socialist candidates entering the chambers, our elected officials still show great poverty of creativity in finding solutions to problems that predate all of us, even as they swell their chests making emotional condemnations the mornings after countless shootings have occurred and body counts been announced.

Added to this political ineptitude are the daily news accounts of shootings in the neighborhoods of Chicago's south and west sides featuring primarily young Black and Latin males. Mainstream media is still a force in forging attitudes. In their "service" of presenting the news, they not only numb the viewers' sensitivity to violence but also, more sinisterly, tighten prejudices of the average citizen. The media's attempts to showcase positive examples within the African American and Latin communities are trivial compared to the litany of vice that digitally shoots across screens and headline stories every day, showing the disproportionate racial profiles of perpetrators.

One only has to reflect on the different characters of both the 2020 George Floyd protests and riots alongside what happened in Kenosha, Wisconsin, that same year and in Washington, D.C., on January 6, 2021. When Black Lives Matter protestors marched in the capital, there were armed soldiers, masked and poised at the Lincoln Memorial and other strategic sites in Washington to quell any violence. An armed, and white, Kyle Rittenhouse marched down the streets of Kenosha, Wisconsin, unmolested by authorities until the shooting stopped. In 2021, the armed crowd, again mainly white and male, that tried to "Stop the Steal" of the 2020 presidential election was all but escorted into the legislature and around the halls and chambers (although there seemed to have been some well-informed people in the group as to areas to infiltrate).

What if the racial identities had been different? What if a seventeen-year-old Black youth had carried a gun down that street in Kenosha? What if armed Black men and women had marched anywhere in Washington and

May Day protestors atop the Haymarket Memorial in 2014, one of whom wears a Guy Fawkes mask—recalling the early seventeenth-century Catholic radicals fighting the British—popularly seen in protests since the 2005 film *V for Vendetta*. *Courtesy of the author.*

attacked any building? Would Kenosha police have let the Black kid get off several rounds of bullets before they intervened? Would the soldiers have let Black protestors breach security at many different stages and levels, waiting a few hours before effectively quelling that insurrection? Would Donald Trump have called them patriots?

There is one other distinction that needs to be highlighted regarding the differences between the Black Live Matter movement and the "J6" insurrection. The 2020 protests and passions of the Black Lives Matter protestors, alongside the rioting in many cities, was another expression of the Black community's frustration over yet another series of killings of men of color. George Floyd's murder, having been witnessed by billions of people throughout the world, became the catalyst for the summer of protest and violence. But what happened on January 6, 2021, was an attempted disruption, not simply of traffic or public transportation as in civil rights–based protests or even "settling scores" against businesses and corporations that sometimes fuels rioting. The violence in Washington, D.C., that day was focused on the actual derailment of the mechanisms of constitutional government. Protesting what one thinks is a stolen election is one thing, but actively and violently working for the upending of the process of a legitimately judged certification process crosses into rebellion.

The Haymarket Eight of 1886 and the Chicago Eight of 1968 charged with murder and conspiracy to riot were convicted on less evidence.

The insurrectionists of January 6 become yet another example of yet another power group's gasping in the centuries-old pattern of clinging to its declining potency. In a preliminary study out of the University of Chicago and using information gleaned from social media, demographics and voting patterns, Austin Wright of the university's Harris School of Public Policy and David Van Dijke of the University of Michigan noted patterns of involvement in the "Stop the Steal" protest and eventual attack on the legislature. Those involved appeared to be people influenced by the Proud Boys group and the ousted social media platform Parler, strong voices among people of the far right and the most likely to feel alienated by "them" gaining more voice in government and society.

The differences of this latest expression of the "we" versus "they" dichotomy are essential to understanding the significance and precariousness of our position as a democratic republic. If this group of citizens insists on clinging to the power that they perceive they are losing, then social harmony will elude us well through this century and the legitimacy of every election will be open to doubt, leaving open the very real possibility of a repeat of

January 6. This group targets "them," the other, as the scapegoat, and this other group is the previously disenfranchised and growing in numbers. The Black and Brown communities are taking their long-awaited rightful places in society after struggling in ways that the established power players (historically, white males) have not had to fight.

We will not get far in racial harmony if we can't even come to an understanding of the legitimacy of the aforementioned critical race theory in addition to accepting that "Black lives matter" is not simply a political slogan. While it's true that all lives matter equally, it is the painful reality of American history that without exception, the lives of African Americans have had to be defended in a way that no other group has had to defend itself. The Native American experience, while abhorrent and inexcusable, is different. The Native people were given a certain level of autonomy and nationhood, even an ability to hold Black slaves, at the same time that the Black slave was denied the recognition of full humanity and the full protection of civil law. No other group has had to fight for basic rights that all others, even the oftentimes despised non-WASP immigrants of Asia alongside southern and eastern Europe. No other group has had to steel itself against the possibility of rising too far, too fast, of being seen as being "uppity," of kowtowing to "Massa" even after emancipation. No other group has had to give "the talk" to its children (*not* the sex talk) before setting them off into a potentially lethal world of running afoul of civil authority.

The ubiquitous power playing of politicians seeks to crush resistance to the "god of the way things are," to restate Jane Addams's indictment, of those who clutch the reins of control, whether their name is Rutherford B. Hayes, Richard J. Daley, James Earl Ray, Donald Trump or Lori Lightfoot. The March of Folly, to borrow from historian Barbara Tuchman, will continue as the march of time progresses, until and only until citizens come to expect a better character of politician and can uphold those who actually express true leadership qualities.

With Bedrolls on Their Backs and Protest in Their Hearts

The spoon-fed lies of the Cold War have spoiled. The domino theory, the assumption that if one country was to "go red" then the entire region would "fall" to communism, was classic paranoid reaction to the rumblings of the growing poor of the world, and it nearly led to mutually assured destruction of "us" and "them." The idiocies that allow us to still live in the real fear of someone "pushing the button" continue to be bandied about by politicians and their military gorillas. This is what alleged leaders of both political parties in the United States have spawned, alongside their communist counterparts in the Soviet Union and China since 1945 and past the demise of the Red Menace since 1989. The legacy of the 1960s protests is that people can still move the seemingly immovable politicians who have held the world hostage.

The ugly reality of the war effort in Vietnam is that American and Soviet involvement wasn't a product of the 1960s. It began shortly after the truce in Korea was signed. French Indo-China, as it was called by the colonizers of southeast Asia, was divided up in the 1954 Geneva Accords between the Soviet Union and the United States (North Vietnam and South Vietnam, respectively), with the western areas of the former French colony being "granted" independence as the Kingdoms of Laos and Cambodia. There may be few things during the Cold War era that are as iconic as the Vietnam War; there is nothing that stands out clearer in that war than the worldwide protests of the late 1960s; and there is nothing of these outcries standing in comparison to the protests in Chicago in late August 1968 during the Democratic National Convention.

The assassinations of the thirty-nine-year-old Martin Luther King and forty-two-year-old Robert Kennedy in less than three months' time marked for the coming-of-age baby boomers the last gasp of hope for change through conventional channels. This is certified by the testimony of several of the "Chicago Seven" (eight by counting Black Panther leader Bobby Seale, who was arrested for contempt of court and was actually handcuffed and gagged during the end of his presence at the trial in 1969). Part of their defense was to show that they had begun to organize the peace rally as early as February 1968, planning to support the nomination of Robert Kennedy with the hopes that a younger face leading at least the Democratic Party would lead to a change of thinking and of government actions. With his death came that shadow of hopelessness known all too well in Black communities throughout the country for the previous one hundred years.

The Democratic Party (along with Republicans) and the City of Chicago were ill-prepared for the angst, the chutzpa, the in-your-face attitude, the utter disregard for their own personal safety or conventional respect for authority that the young protestors possessed that summer. Gathering in the north side neighborhoods of Lincoln Park and Old Town for the

Festival of Life beginning on Saturday, August 24, 1968, hippies, yippies, flower children, love-in devotees and observers made a statement against the "Festival of Death" that was being waged in southeast Asia as well as throughout the inner cities of America.

The Chicago History Museum hosted a yearlong exhibit in 2014–15 of the 1968 events, and Brian Mullgardt wrote of the vibrant activism of the neighborhoods in his article "The Park Is Ours" for the magazine *Chicago History*. The pattern of the weekend was to set the template for the next three days, culminating in the now-iconic show of force and resistance between the Chicago Police Department, Mayor Daley and the protestors in Grant Park. Small gatherings had begun on Saturday, and the police left the attendees alone until 11:00 p.m. when the city curfew was enforced in Lincoln Park. Fires were doused, people were escorted out of the park and that first evening ended in peace. By Sunday, the festive mood had returned, as the main bulk of the crowds formed and then stayed, in spite of the curfew. Police moved in and began the dispersal, this time in larger numbers and swinging nightsticks according to much testimony both at the Chicago Seven trial and in reports the following day by some of the newspapers.

Chanting began as people left: "Parks to the people," and "Let's go to the streets." The Love-In turned protest march that Sunday night and poured into the streets of the Old Town neighborhood and, according to witnesses, jammed traffic all along the north- and southbound streets of Clark, Wells and Lincoln. This pattern would repeat on Monday evening as well, although that night marked the beginning of what would culminate infamously two days later. The occupiers of Lincoln Park would not leave when so ordered. Barricades were built, bonfires were lit in trash cans and the protestors began to gather anything to throw at the approaching police. One more warning to vacate the park was given, and then tear gas cannisters were thrown. Ministers from various denominations were present to counsel calm; some received a clubbing, and many gave firsthand accounts of the mêlée to newspapers and at the 1969 trial.

Tuesday brought a calm during the day, pleas from community leaders to neighborhood residents to allow protestors safe haven that night should the curfew again be enforced and more speeches. In one of the few instances of individual leaders stepping up, Bobby Seale and Jerry Rubin addressed the crowd and would suffer the wrath of the court for it the next year at the trial. Otherwise, it was a from the ground up protest that was rooted in Chicagoans and others taking a stand against the play-by-our-rules-or-else attitude of city officials.

That night, the curfew was enforced again with a twist of brutality unknown previously in Chicago: the police brought in mace-spraying trucks and introduced "federal streamer gas" to the crowd. The effect of the streamer gas is that, unlike tear gas, it sticks to grass, skin and clothing, causing burning of the skin and vomiting. In spite of the presence of almost two hundred clergy, the planting of a ten-foot cross in the park and the singing of religious songs, the police advanced and cleared the park with the chemical weapons and their ubiquitous nightsticks.

The events of Wednesday evening in the downtown Grant Park are notorious. From the accounts of on-the-ground reporters and film crews to protestors, Mayor Daley and Senator Abraham Ribicoff of Connecticut, the words and actions sped across the globe and into the convention hall. Film crews, reporters and protestors were beaten and gassed. Ribicoff announced in his nomination speech of George McGovern that with a McGovern presidency, "We wouldn't have Gestapo tactics in the streets of Chicago." According to accounts, especially the reporting of a professional lip reader hired by one of the non-machine newspapers, Daley shouted, "Fuck you, you Jew son of a bitch, you lousy motherfucker, go home." His obscenities and heckling were combined with those of his sons (one of them was future mayor Richard M. Daley) along with those of his staffers and most of the Illinois convention delegation.

A clear analysis of the background of and buildup to the convention is given by Bill and Lori Granger in their *Lords of the Last Machine: The Story of Politics in Chicago*. To sum up an entire system that stretches through decades and is now in its third century, Chicago officials, they write, were defending themselves "in a traditional way: by attack. It is the only possible defense in the game of politics as it is played in Chicago." In the end, this all too often used tactic oversaw the deployment of twelve thousand police officers on twelve-hour shifts, six thousand army soldiers, another few thousand members of the Illinois National Guard, Illinois state troopers, FBI agents and the Secret Service. In a stretch of four miles, a force of about twenty-five thousand was deployed. Old methods reap the same old results, just as they did in 1855, 1877 and 1886. Students of history who show up to class could propose different solutions and, dare one say, tactics, but in 1968 the muscle that was flexed was the bloodiest and witnessed by the most people globally ever recorded in the city.

While there was enough responsibility to go around for what happened, the powerholders placed the blame squarely on the shoulders of the protestors. The scapegoats that were needed to expunge any guilt from

The fasces, adorning the entryways of Chicago's City Hall since 1906, symbolizes civil authority's power of punishment (the bundle of rods) and execution (the axe) since ancient Roman times. *Courtesy of Jyoti Srivastava.*

Chicago's political elite and the oft-used muscle of the Chicago Police Department were provided in the figures of David Dellinger, Rennie Davis, Tom Hayden, Abbie Hoffman, Jerry Rubin, Lee Weiner, John Froines and Bobby Seale. The trial transcripts make for great comedy, save for the fact that the prosecution was so tragically misdirected. The trial succeeded in a system exonerating itself, granting immunity for the city's chief of state and writing him a political pass for the next eight years that he sat in office. The grim reaper in 1976 was the only one to dislodge him from the throne.

Many of Chicago's newspapers share the responsibility for their role in fanning the flames of fear and paranoia in a city already on edge by the energy of youth and organized protest since the late 1950s. A pro-establishment journalism stoked the fires with unsubstantiated stories of assassination plans targeting Mayor Daley, the Democratic candidates and delegates and police officers. These reports certainly played a part in the construction of a highly militarized, nervous, trigger-fingered, muscle-flexing atmosphere that greeted convention delegates and protestors.

Rather than relying on the same "tough on crime" posturing that has marked the actions of monarchs, dictators, presidents and mayors for centuries—Chicago is not exceptional in this regard—what would've happened had the city granted permits for the use of public space, at least in the Lincoln Park and Old Town neighborhoods, for the weekend and the first few days of the week? The concentration of protestors and festival attendees could have been contained in a small area, easily monitored, if that was a major concern of the officials. Most likely, there might have been little, if any, crowd-rushing into the neighboring streets. Even if the permitted use of Grant Park downtown that saw the largest show of force could have been acquired, there may have been little violence for officials to deal with. What if the mayor, the parks commissioner and city council members had set up communication with groups of clergy and other neighborhood leaders who had offered to serve as intermediaries before and during that final week of August?

In the words of Bob Dylan in 1963, his prophecies and admonitions ignored:

> *Come senators, congressmen, please head the call.*
> *Don't stand in the doorway, don't block up the hall.*
> *For he that gets hurt will be he who has stalled.*
> *There's a battle outside and it's ragin'.*
> *It'll soon shake your windows and rattle your walls.*
> *For the times they are a changin'.*

The Girls, the Gays and the Theys

Lorraine Hansberry, writing with the initials LHN (her married name being Nemiroff) in the lesbian-focused journal *The Ladder*'s May 1957 issue, commended them:

> *You are obviously serious people and I feel that women, without wishing to foster any* **separatist** [emphasis in original] *notions, homo or hetero, indeed have a need for their own publications and organizations.... What ought to be clear is that one is oppressed or discriminated against because one is different.... This is perhaps the bitterest of the entire pill.*

In the aftermath of the nationwide Red Hunts of the early 1950s, communists and "pinkoes" were still suspect, as they had been since the 1886 Haymarket Bombing and especially since the Russian Revolution in 1917. Added to this motley mix of Moscow's minions were those in the entertainment industries and, most particularly, homosexuals. Even though in many large cities, the gay, lesbian and trans community, impersonators and dancers were tolerated if enough kickback money was presented to mob enforcers (sometimes with police badges), the overall attitudes of society were suspicious of this ne'er-do-well group of others. Officially, the U.S. government's harassment policy of homosexual citizens was rooted in the fear that "our" enemies could use "them" to gain state secrets through blackmail, threatening to out the person, ruining their lives and shaming their families if their so-called perversions became known.

A telling report in the ever-judgmental *Chicago Tribune* by reporter Willard Edwards in 1950 speaks of the issue based on stereotyping and shabby historical analysis:

> *History discloses that the rise to power of such men* [homosexuals] *has frequently been a problem disturbing rulers. They are often ambitious men of intellectual attainments, attracting others of their like, forming an influential clique which strives to shape policy to its own ends. Such men have a fatal weakness when occupying positions of trust with access to confidential records. They are subject to blackmail through exposure of their sordid practices and thus may be induced to furnish foreign agents with their country's secrets.*

In other words, apparently "Mary" can't keep her mouth shut!

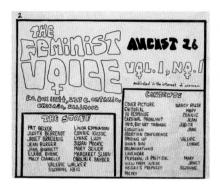

The cover of the first issue of *The Feminist Voice. Courtesy of Loyola University's Woman's Leadership Archive.*

So, herein lies the core of the issue: members of society, individuals, church leadership and politicians all give rise to that society's attitudes. Thoughts, beliefs and prejudices all come from human beings and are not created by a nameless, faceless society or grand It. Human beings who hold to a different sense of sexual orientation or gender expression can be made to feel a certain way by other members of the same society who hold a dominant view of sexuality. The danger then is not that the Soviet Union could have found out about government officials being gay, and thereby possessing blackmailing power over them; the real issue is why the outing of the government official would make any difference at all in the alleged leading nation of the so-called free world. If there were not the real shame, threat of job loss, destruction of family relationships and criminal prosecution connected with the truth of someone's sexual identity, then there would be no real threat of blackmail.

A 1919 German film, *Different from the Others*, was co-written by Richard Oswald and gay activist Magnus Hirschfeld. The main character is a violinist who falls in love with his male student, and after being found out, he is blackmailed. After paying the extortionist, the violinist takes him to court, and the musician's homosexuality is publicized. So shunned, he commits suicide. The final words of the film express Hirschfeld's work in Germany that he had begun before the First World War:

> *You have to keep living…to change the prejudices by which this man has been made one of the countless victims.…Restore the honor of this man and bring justice to him, and to all those who came before him, and all those to come after him.*

The movie ends with the infamous Paragraph 175 of the 1871 German Criminal Code, which made homosexual acts illegal in the newly founded German Reich, being crossed out of a law book. The film was banned in Germany, but its optimism makes it one of the earliest and boldest statements against oppression of homosexuality recorded. And as the Nazis brought the legislation to the fore in one of their many tactics to promote the fertilization of women for the propagation of the master race, they used the pink triangle to set homosexuals apart in the concentration camps. And even though the German government would not grant reparations to homosexual survivors of the death camps as they rightly granted the Jewish survivors, and in spite of the fact that Germany would not nullify Paragraph 175 until 1994, Hirschfeld still stands as the strongest voice of his time in Europe and the United States for recognition of the "love that dare not speak its name."

Legislation on the federal, state and local levels across the United States reinforced by homophobia and bigotry all led to the codification of the dominant views on sexuality, gender identification, behavior and even dress. Within the first decade of statehood, Illinois further tightened its laws against sodomy with the 1827 expansion of the legislation: criminal penalties included loss of citizenship through the prohibition of voting and jury service. The so-called crimes against nature (as homosexual acts were commonly called) would remain law until the revision of the state's criminal code in 1961, when those acts "performed in private by consenting adults" were removed from the books. It was, in the words of St. Sukie de la Croix in *Chicago Whispers: A History of LGBTQ Chicago before Stonewall*, "the first crack in the armor of the nation's institutionalized homophobia." But, like the passage of the Thirteenth, Fourteenth and Fifteenth Amendments to the U.S. Constitution after the Civil War relating to the freedom and enfranchisement of those formerly enslaved and their progeny, a change in legislation doesn't necessarily mean a change of heart or behavior of the dominant group.

Cultural attitudes toward homosexuality in the Black community, biases and condemnations that have extended into the twenty-first century, are deeply rooted. Though the Roaring Twenties of pre–Great Depression Chicago were years marked by much tolerance, the reality in the entertainment industries at the time, especially in the bars and lounges known for same-sex dancing and cross-dressing impersonators, was still one that ran the risk of exposure to the outside world. Before World War I, Chicago's south side boasted a lively jazz and ragtime nightlife in clubs like the Pekin Theater, De Luxe and the Dreamland Ballroom, all playing host to an interracial mix that could have served as testimony to the benefits of the type of permissiveness that welcomed those whom the rest of society deemed perverts. In *Chicago Whispers*, de la Croix showcases these and many other gay/lesbian/trans-friendly establishments that thrived in the city's Black neighborhoods.

On the north side, in 1924, World War I veteran Henry Gerber established the Society for Human Rights in Lincoln Park and began publishing the newsletter *Friendship and Freedom* for the gay, lesbian and trans community in Chicago. Neighborhood pressure forced the closure of the office and printing efforts after a police raid. Even though the block showcased two brothels on either end of the street, the existence of the first support network and outreach for "them" was too much of a blush for the pallid residents of the neighborhood.

Gerber survived the horror of war on the battlefields of the western front, kept up the pretense of being "straight" so as to earn an honorable discharge from the military and chose exile on the East Coast to more fighting in Chicago for rights for which he and others had risked their lives. The hypocrisy of the military's ban on gay soldiers, most ridiculously articulated in the Clinton administration's notorious "Don't Ask, Don't Tell" policy of 1993, was finally ended in 2011, exonerating generations of service personnel who had been dishonorably discharged solely on the basis of their sexual orientation. Chicago boasts one of the earliest memorials to LGBTQ members of the community who served in the military. At the northwest corner of Addison and Halsted Streets stands a simple granite pillar with a pink triangle above an inscription and wreathed "With Liberty and Justice for All."

An Illinois senate commission was established in 1967 to study "the problem of homosexuality in the state." Again, *they* are the problem that *we* must solve. The study, passing the state senate with a bipartisan vote of 30–8, expressed the tired social majority view that "they were contaminating youth" and are "clearly misfits." In the words of Democrat James Loukas, basking in the glory that he imagined, "Homosexuals are organized and are a cancer on our society....The dissolution of the glory that was once Greece was caused basically by homosexualism." Republican Joseph Krasowski echoed his colleague's indefatigable ignorance with a contemporary (and self-righteously personal) anecdote: "Homosexuals do bother people. It is embarrassing. I have been approached myself on the streets of Chicago. My big concern is teenagers being contaminated by this way of life."

The Chicago City Council took up the issue of gay rights legislation in the spring of 1974 but referred the issue to a subcommittee of the Judiciary Committee to avoid voting on anything close to granting civil protections against job loss, loss of child custody, unlawful arrests in bars and the subsequent public shaming in the press. Heavily pressured by the firefighters' union (odd, one might say) and the Catholic Church (not surprising, one could add) in the city, it was debated safely in subcommittee and not brought to the full Judiciary Committee for a vote to bring it before the whole council. African American Leslie Trotter, a gay activist in the city, wrote in *The Defender*, reviewing the votes of four Black council members:

> *I wish to express my support for and faith in Ald. Timothy C. Evans (4ᵗʰ) and Ald. Anna R. Langford (16ᵗʰ) for having the courage to stand up for the rights of gay people and send the so-called Gay Rights Bill back in the Chicago City Council. However, I was appalled by the actions of Pro Tempore Wilson Frost (34ᵗʰ) and William H. Shannon (17ᵗʰ) who did not support the bill....I am not trying to argue the merits of gay liberation or gay people but since the persons named are black it does seem they would give support to this other oppressed group. Homosexuality is not a white or black thing. [However] it is a people's thing. Therefore, we must act with courage to end this vestige of oppression.*

The bust of Mayor Harold Washington (*Abelardo Ghoulam, artist*) at the main branch of the Chicago Public Library, the Harold Washington Branch, at Van Buren and State Streets. *Courtesy of the author.*

The Human Rights Ordinance would pass in the Chicago City Council in December 1988, thanks in large part to the words and actions of the city's first African American mayor and LGBTQ ally, Harold Washington, who died the year before the ordinance passed under the caretaking of his successor, Eugene Sawyer. The State of Illinois rescinded its sexual orientation–based discriminatory laws in 2005 under Governor Rod Blagojevich.

Prejudice runs deep and it cuts an old path, but suppression gives birth to new strength in people. In spite of lively anti-vice activities in pre– and post–World War I Chicago, the underground lives and entertainments of those whose love dare not speak its name were vibrant. Entertainers in both Black and white neighborhoods in the city found new expression through music and dance, through early drag shows and cross-dressing impersonators and especially through the camaraderie of simply being together with others who shared one's own views and lifestyles. While police raids were something that became major points of contention between authorities and the early gay and lesbian populations, it wasn't until the 1960s (especially after the 1969 Stonewall Uprising in New York City) that it became intolerable in the Windy City.

But prior to that, raids were a constant threat, looming just beyond the entrance to the bar, lounge or club that catered to a primarily gay, lesbian or trans crowd. In addition to criminal prosecution for "public indecency" (same-sex hand-holding, kissing, solicitation and conversation), "lewd behavior" (same-sex dancing or kissing), "cross-dressing" and other hazy classifications of "perversion," the patrons of these establishments, upon arrest inside the place, could be greeted on the street by cameramen and reporters from any of the city's several daily newspapers that feasted on the publicizing of names, addresses and employers of the arrestees. It could mean the real possibility of criminal prosecution, job loss, divorce, loss of child custody in the cases of lesbians and an increase in suicide, which the same newspapers reported on with a macabre relish.

In 1949, at the dawn of the American scapegoating of the gay, lesbian and trans communities in its god-blessed war on the communist conspiracy, the *Tribune* wrote under the headline "Tower Ticker" of the Windup Lounge, "The wind up at the Windup, [669 N.] State Street, sin den where boy met boy before Police Captain [Thomas] Harrison raided it, proves that the lower the lights, the greater the scandal power."

The tactic would become standard operating procedure as it had in many major cities: plainclothesmen stood at the door of the Windup, allowing people inside. They observed small groups of men congregating, announced the raid and proceeded to make arrests, escorting them out in front of photographers who just happened to be waiting outside. In February 1952, the *Tribune* reported, "Police charged [that] the place is a hangout for perverts. They said women generally were attired in men's clothing [cross-dressing, according to the city's ordinance] and were dancing together. The men…were consorting with one another." Later, it reported, "Thirty-nine men and a woman were arrested last night in a police raid.…Detectives… said they found two men kissing each other at the bar and saw several other men dancing with each other." And yet again, the paper conspired in the public shaming of the arrestees by publicizing their personal information.

Of course, the unpleasantries could be avoided if the owners of the targeted establishments could join with other wise proprietors and donate to the neighborhood mafia boss or mob-backed police officer in the precinct every month for the added "security" of the premises. As society relegated gay bars to the darkness, the intersection of "Queerborn" (Dearborn Street) and "Perversion" (Division Street) became *the* gay district on the near northside from the end of World War II through the 1960s.

In the typical hypocrisy of the state-approved administrators of sleaze, the mobsters and their cohorts in the Chicago Police Department controlled bars such as the Shoreline 7 on West Division, known to be "syndicate-owned" in the community, with a back room that was a "haven for police captains, mobsters, and politicians." It wouldn't be until the June 1973 federal indictments of Captain Clarence Braasch and forty-seven police officers from three districts for extortion of many gay-owned bars that things loosened, even if it was just a bit. In the end, Braasch and twenty-two officers were convicted of "convincing" owners to join their "Vice Club" for a mere $100 a month (just over $600 per month in 2021 purchasing power), which was split between the captain and the assigned officers.

Added to the hypocrisy of the generous mafia thugs and their guard dogs wearing badges (the same badges that other officers died wearing while actually doing their jobs) was the condescending paternalism of "father knows best" American society in the 1950s that was exposed (and ignored) in the ridiculous displays of the courts reviewing obscenity laws. Cases involved debate between lawyers and were presided over by judges to decide the meaning of "excessive genital delineation" in a model's posing strap, be they male or female, or impersonating one or the other. It was the precursor of the circus atmosphere of the 1990s senate hearings on the nomination of Clarence Thomas to the Supreme Court and the presence of pubic hairs on the judge's soda can and the impeachment hearings of President William Clinton showcasing a semen-stained dress as well as the meanings of the words *is* and *sexual relations*. Puritans seem to go to great lengths to protect the public, even to the extent of farce.

Guardians of morality were active in Chicago from the early part of the twentieth century's battles against the prostitution of the Levee District on South Dearborn Street and against the "wets" during the Prohibition era, but from the mid-1950s onward, "anti-smut" groups were particularly vigilant against the entertainment and arts communities that supported impersonators, cross-dressers and same-sex photography collections. From 1959 to 1961, there was a passionate nationwide debate on the issues of obscenity.

Chicago anti-smut campaigners threw a wide dragnet across the city, aiming efforts at newsstand operators first. On October 8, 1960, fifty newsstand operators were arrested for possessing and selling pornographic material. Fifteen were actually convicted. On January 17, 1961, fifty-three staffers and members of the Adonis Male Club were arrested for violating the U.S. Post Office's ban on sending obscene material through the mail. The proprietors had set up a members only yearbook with names, contact information and interests whereby those who joined could then contact each other—a type of pre-digital dating app. The USPS saw it differently. The Oak Park husband-and-wife cofounders were convicted and sentenced to one year and a day in prison, with three years of probation. The arrests were highly publicized, as were identifying details of the arrestees, which led once again to job loss, family turmoil and even an attempted murder (one arrestee was injured in a hit and-run "accident") alongside several suicides reported in July 1965 by the *Tribune*.

Given the commonality of these types of stories of raid and prosecution across the cities of this country and many other nations, it might be seen as being quite remarkable that an uprising like the one at the Stonewall Inn in New York City's Greenwich Village didn't occur earlier than 1969. It's probable, though, that one of the main reasons, and quite possibly the strongest, for the long-standing suffering, of submitting to the abuse for so long, was the fear of being outed. No one had to be convinced of the consequences of publicly being known as gay or lesbian and even as trans: at best, if one received a compassionate response, it was probably in the form of a coaxing to get professional psychiatric help, therapy for the disturbance of same-sex attractions. In 1974, substituting "homosexuality" with "sexual orientation disturbance" and then in 1987, removing even that, the American Psychiatric Association seemingly removed same-sex attraction itself from the list of psychiatric illnesses. While still listing "sexual disorder not otherwise specified" as a diagnosis into the twenty-first century, a relatively unified APA in 2013 removed any diagnostic category that can be based on any sexual orientation.

But people will adapt, they will bide their time, they will adjust and they will survive in creative ways. The enslaved population developed music, song and dreams of freedom that morphed into active pursuits of escape, rebellion, the development of the Underground Railroad and a constant push for full freedom and civil rights that extends into our own day. Similarly, the LGBTQ community, over the decades and under different monikers of GL, LGB and any other combinations of letters that people use to express themselves, has cowered and stood tall, cowered again and stood stronger. After yet more disgraces, it has risen even higher with the "Don't Say Gay" reactionism that brings the old "love that dare not speak its name" into our own day.

But all of it comes with a price; all of it comes only after long suffering and ultimately with enough people at some point saying, "Enough is enough." It has taken four centuries for this nation to even begin the conversation on the reckoning that needs to happen regarding the legacy of slavery. While the social acceptance of homosexuality may be a foregone conclusion at the moment, it does not have the guarantee of permanence. This has been witnessed regarding the women's rights movement, seen since early 2022 with the unprecedented leaking of the Supreme Court's opinions and renderings of the abortion and related privacy issues.

Chicago activist Bob Sloane expressed the will of the community of all with respect to orientation, skin color and gender in a 1964 letter to the editor of the *Tribune* as well an open letter to Republican senator Everett Dirksen (aka "The Wizard of Ooze"): "Let's get in step with history. Have the courage to extend equal rights to all Americans. Let's become a first-class country by eliminating second class citizenship." In addition to the growing calls for recognition and the ongoing pressure for full decriminalization of behavior still considered deviant under city ordinances such as cross-dressing and the usual same-sex activities of kissing, talking and holding hands, the gay, lesbian and trans voice was growing.

Language and word choice play a large role in the ongoing struggles of any group, as well as those who oppose them. Too often, highly impassioned vocabulary is used in news stories and individual arguments that betray one's biases and do little to open lines of communication for resolutions of differences. *Mattachine Midwest*, an early publication of the community, wrote through the pen of editor David Stienecker to the *Chicago Daily News*, thanking the paper for its fair treatment of the magazine but challenging reporters on their sensationalism and prejudicial language: "Stereotyped and biased phrasing such as 'deviates' and 'bizarre double-life' shed no new light on the subject."

With the uprising of the trans, gay and lesbian communities on June 28, 1969, at the Stonewall Inn in New York City came the first and ongoing rising up of the entire LGBTQ population. While some remained closeted well into the next century, the community as a whole marks this date as the beginning of the end of those doors staying shut. In Chicago, protests didn't reach the violent clashes as happened at Stonewall, but by the first anniversary of the event, organizers had put together protests downtown in support of the outing that was long overdue, of an end to discriminatory laws and ordinances in the city and the state, as well as of an affirmation of the lifestyle that had been long present and long suppressed. This was all prior to floats and bands and politicians waving safely in parades up and down North Halsted, the area formerly known as Boystown. Police were still raiding bars, and the names of arrestees were still being publicized in the newspaper through the 1970s and well into the '80s, with job and child custody losses still real and legal.

Small protests outside bars and in the press continued as the city and Cook County, led by Sheriff (later Governor) Richard Ogilvie, stepped up efforts of harassment and shaming. By the mid-1960s, the county had led raids in the western suburbs of gay bars, most notoriously the 1964 raid of Louis Gage's Lounge, netting the arrests of hundreds of gay, lesbian and cross-dressing patrons and providing the papers with the usual fare of names, addresses and workplaces of the arrestees. In 1972, the Advocates of Gay Action published a leaflet for the upcoming elections in the city, state and nation. "Lick 3 Dicks" was the battle cry to oust Governor Richard Ogilvie, Mayor Richard J. Daley and President Richard Nixon, with Ogilvie being the only one to lose reelection.

The first open (read *out*) gay/lesbian march in the city of Chicago occurred on April 15, 1970, at Civic Center Plaza (Daley Plaza) in anticipation of the first anniversary of the Stonewall Uprising. The *Daily News* covered it and noted the unifying spirit of both anti-war and women's liberation groups alongside the LGBT banners. Some of the lesbian protestors peeled off and joined other women who confronted celebrity guests of Hugh Heffner at the Playboy Mansion attending a $100/ticket ($650 in 2021 purchasing power) anti-war fundraiser, challenging misogyny in the press. They were ignored, with one celebrity claiming that it wasn't a woman's issue, as "men were dying in Vietnam, not women." The protesting spirit can be selective and really wrong. Within a year, more marches and rallies would advocate for "spreading claustrophobia," an escape from the closet for the gay and lesbian community, as stated by the Northern Illinois University Gay Liberation Front's first regional convention in 1971.

One of the most horrific episodes in the tragedy that has resulted from race-based bigotry in the trans community in Chicago occurred in November 1970. James Clay, a twenty-four-year-old Black man and cross-dresser with a criminal record was shot by two Chicago police officers as he fled from them after apparently being spotted soliciting someone in a car. He ran into a building, pulled out a knife and was shot eight times in the head and abdomen by the officers who apprehended him. There was an outcry in the transvestite and gay/lesbian community as well as within the Black community as a whole, uniting with the Black Panther Party in protests against the ongoing harassment, surveillance and setup tactics of the Chicago Police Department and Federal Bureau of Investigation. The Chicago Gay Alliance petitioned the FBI to investigate the incident for civil rights violations, but the bureau found that "the evidence did not warrant prosecution by the Civil Rights Division."

Pressure on the city and the police department to address the harassment at gay bars continued over the next several years, and protests outside some of the bars themselves kept up the pressure against the racist practice of checking the identification of some customers (Black) more stringently, while allowing others (white) inside with fewer proofs of age. Divisions in the community as well as efforts to heal rifts have challenged it even into 2020. But things do improve, as was witnessed in the bold step of the Boystown neighborhood agreeing to a name change (North Halsted) in the wake of the statue-busting months following much of the protests and riots of that summer: "Boystown" had come to imply young, male (historically white) and fit and so supports, at least inadvertently, a racist, ageist, misogynistic, body-shaming aura. Steps such as these go far in changing perceptions with both small gestures and grand ones.

By the onset of the AIDS epidemic in the early 1980s, a stronger racial alliance had tightened, and this allowed the community to march into the twenty-first century more unified than ever and in spite of the incapacity and unwillingness of the federal government to confront the health crisis as it began. With the virus disproportionately ravaging Black and Brown communities in this country, it became more important for gay men of color to have safe spaces to come out publicly. The cultural closeting that has been so strong in these communities sealed many lips, and that silence has extorted a high price in lives. (The ongoing labeling of monkeypox as yet another "gay disease" in the twenty-first century has further alienated men who might seek care early and creates a naïve population of any orientation.)

Positive steps that were taken as a result of the AIDS crisis were in efforts like the formation of Black and White Men Together in 1980 and especially the Marches on Washington for gay rights that had been occurring since the first in 1979 to commemorate the tenth anniversary of Stonewall. By the late 1980s, the annual event had grown significantly, fueled by the passions and deaths related to the AIDS crisis. The growing strength of the entire LGBTQ community has led to an expansion of the understanding of the umbrella term *gay rights* and has come to encompass everything from the erasure of orientation-based discrimination, adoption rights, custody rights, marriage equality, gender identification and honesty in education ("Just Say Gay").

If the lack of immediate federal response to the onset of AIDS in the United States was not due to negligence or outright malice, then it was the result of a woefully inadequate healthcare system that, throughout the next four decades, culminated in the criminal incompetence of the Trump and Biden administrations during the COVID-19 pandemic. These health disasters have exposed the worthlessness of the politicians of both capitalist parties as well as the criminal deficiencies of the profit-based healthcare system they so passionately defend and to which American citizens so ignorantly and obstinately cling as "the best in the world."

The story of Latin Chicago with regard to the LGBTQ community needs much more research. One of the first to delve into the treasure-trove is John D'Emilio in his *Queer Legacies: Stories from Chicago's LGBTQ Archive*. In addition to the cultural stigma of sexual attraction and expression that deviated from the norm, there was the pressure of one's religious upbringing to contend with, especially in the Black and Latin communities. Nothing stronger has come about in the closing years of the twentieth century than the formation of Amigas Latinas in 1995, which began as a Sunday brunch group and grew into a community hub to support the growing outing of women in Latin Chicago. It would last for a decade and close in the bittersweet realization that the group had birthed stronger women who were taking active roles in the day-to-day life of the city as fully active citizens of Chicago and not as fringe members of the lesbian community.

Prejudices are fed by ignorance; ignorance is bred through stereotypes and a lack of experiences. Education and exposure are the best tools to dismantle prejudices of any kind. How we speak about issues and people is important. In addition to our own words and the language of news media, of which hard copy or digital is a major source of information for a large number of people, the role of churches has been significant in the ongoing tension and debate regarding gay rights. Members of the LGBTQ community in our own day still struggle with the issue of acceptance in the religious traditions of this country: even though many individuals have chosen to reject such convictions, especially in reaction to the established denominations' rejections of different lifestyles, some seek and have found inclusion in the more liberal end of religious traditions.

However, churchgoers of all denominations would be well humbled to learn about the people who have been ostracized over the past decades and centuries due to judgment and censure and who continue to shy away from creeds that perpetuate exclusion by the use of vocabulary such as "objective disorder" and "intrinsic moral evil." Conservativism in the traditionalist Protestant and Catholic theologies has prohibited homosexual actions by church law, claiming biblical precedent and longstanding tradition. Alongside centuries-old teachings is the not-so-subtle church culture that forced "them" into a closet that most churchgoers could never know, or at least admit to. The live-and-let-live creed is difficult to accept when one is tasked with the mission of preaching to all nations and using force to underscore it. What must be remembered is that the preaching of love is to be done partly through word and partly through deed. And the deeds must be in accord with the deeds of the Jewish carpenter who didn't force anyone to do anything, aside from kicking bankers out of a temple on one occasion.

While there is much to be done on both sides of the communion rail regarding religion and homosexuality, individual members of churches and their pastors, alongside the LGBTQ community, would better serve and be better served with an openness to one another as persons. There is a Catholic parish in the North Halsted neighborhood that has a beautiful grassy courtyard next to the church with a fountain in the center. The parish received a lot of publicity in 2018 after it protested to Pride Parade organizers and the city regarding the changing of the parade's start time on the last Sunday of June, from 2:00 p.m. to 12:00, as it would "interfere with the noon Mass."

Rather than issuing the protest, what would happen if, even in the 2020s and moving forward, the parish would cancel this one service, once a year, and open its courtyard as a resting station for parade-goers? What would be morally unacceptable with handing out water or having volunteers staffing a tent with medical personnel on hand for temperature-related concerns? Small actions of kindness and, dare one say, "Christian charity" would go far to heal a lot of wounds and divisions in both communities. Solutions come from people who take initiative and not from elected officials who, as has been shown, rarely act first.

EVERYONE GETS A SEAT
ON THE BUS, BUT WE GET ONLY ONE SEAT EACH!

To an avid user of public transportation, there is little else related to sharing space on a train or bus that is more irksome than someone taking up more than one seat. Whether someone's shopping bag, briefcase or purse is on the seat or whether their whole body is stretched out across four seats, social harmony is more easily attainable with everyone taking only that which has been promised to all. This extends especially in society, when, in its search for peaceful coexistence, we struggle to find solutions on the one hand to the literal problem of one person taking up multiple seats (think of the ongoing plagues of homelessness, untreated mental illness and addictions of all kinds that cause public transportation to be used as shelter) and on the other hand, the metaphorical attitude of the entitled who reach for more than is needed and actually belongs to someone else.

A seat on a train/bus is a good metaphor in the ongoing analysis of the issues and problems of past and present life anywhere in which human beings have decided to live. One of the principles of organized society has been to construct a place, under law, where a variety of people can live together in relative harmony. Problems have occurred when one group feels slighted in this regard, or when one group feels threatened by others around them, or when an established group exerts its preferences in a way that excludes others from the regular processes of government or the general pursuit of happiness.

The tragedy of Chicago's history regarding groups of people has been a sad repetition of such exclusion—the "we" and "they" clashes. But don't be mistaken: this book, while focusing on a lot of upheaval, was written out of a deep love for this city and its people (even its politicians!). The idea for this book was born out of the experiences of everyone around the world since the beginning of 2020, most particularly the people of Chicago. They have shown this author the necessity of further reflection on the challenges facing contemporary society. The troubles of this city today are born out of the troubles of the past, and it is the exclusionary patterns of the powerful against the "other" that is the consistent thread running through our centuries of turbulence.

It is the intention of this book to showcase some pivotal events in Chicago's storm-tossed history, as part of the ongoing struggle of all human beings across the globe trying to live together amid various and sometimes conflicting dreams and expectations. We may have differing goals, and these may even be in mutual opposition, but there is middle ground; there is the possibility of one recognizing that "I can't have it all" but that "I" can settle for some of it so that someone else can have some of it as well. And it doesn't matter what the "it" is, as long as it doesn't infringe on someone else's rights, just as I don't want my rights infringed upon. Again, one can move their "stuff" off the seat next to them so that someone else can sit down, and the one moving their things off the extra seat is still getting the space for which they paid.

WORKS CITED

Addams, Jane. *Twenty Years at Hull-House: 1890–1910*. New York: New American Library, 1960.

Alighieri, Dante. *Inferno*. Translated by James Clive. London: Liveright, 2016.

Boone, Levi. "Inauguration Speech." March 15, 1855. Housed at the Chicago History Museum.

De la Croix, St. Sukie. *Chicago Whispers*. Madison: University of Wisconsin Press, 2013.

———. *Chicago After Stonewall*. Cathedral City, CA: Rattling Good Yarn Press, 2021.

D'Emilio, John. *Queer Legacies: Stories from Chicago's LGBTQ Archives*. Chicago: University of Chicago Press, 2020.

Digital Chicago. *Drag in the Windy City: Black Panthers and the Chicago Gay Alliance*. www.digitalchicagohistory.org.

Duncan, Mike. *The Storm Before the Storm: The Beginning of the End of the Roman Republic*. New York: Public Affairs, 2017.

Flinn, John J. *History of the Chicago Police*. Chicago: Chicago Historical Society, 1887.

Granger, Bill, and Lori Granger. *Lords of the Last Machine: The Story of Politics in Chicago*. New York: Random House, 1987.

Hannah-Jones, Nikole. *The 1619 Project*. New York: One World, 2021.

Hertz, Daniel Kay. *The Battle of Lincoln Park: Urban Renewal and Gentrification in Chicago*. Cleveland, OH: Belt Publishing, 2018.

Hogan, John F. *The 1937 Chicago Steel Strike: Blood on the Prairie.* Charleston, SC: The History Press, 2014.

Hogan, John F., and Brady, Judy E. *The Great Chicago Beer Riot.* Charleston, SC: The History Press, 2015.

In Re Debs. 158 U.S. 564 (1895) 7 May 1895. www.supreme.justia.com.

Jefferson, Thomas. "Query XVIII: Manners." *Notes on the State of Virginia.* London: John Stockdale, 1787. www.teachingamericanhistory.org/documents.

Kelly, Jack. *The Edge of Anarchy.* New York: St. Martin's Press, 2019.

Levine, Mark, et al., eds. *The Official Transcript of the Trial of the Chicago 7.* New York: Simon and Schuster, 2020.

Measuring Worth. www.measuringworth.com.

Michaeli, Ethan. *The Defender: How the Legendary Black Newspaper Changed America.* Boston: Mariner Books, 2016.

Mullgardt, Brian. "The Park Is Ours." *Chicago History* 39, no. 3 (Fall 2014).

Nelson, Otto M. *The Chicago Relief and Aid Society, 1850–1874.* Housed at the Chicago History Museum.

Rousseau, Jean-Jacques. *A Discourse on Inequality.* Translated by Maurice Cranston. New York: Viking Penguin, 1984.

Rulli, Joseph Anthony. *The Chicago Haymarket Affair: A Guide to a Labor Rights Milestone.* Charleston, SC: The History Press, 2016.

———. *Chicago Socialism: The People's History.* Charleston, SC: The History Press, 2019.

Smith, Carl. *Urban Disorder and the Shape of Belief.* Chicago: University of Chicago Press, 1995.

The State of Illinois, 18th General Assembly, concluded January 3, 1853. *General Laws of the State of Illinois.* Springfield, IL: Lanphier and Walker, 1853.

The United States Strike Commission. *Report on the Chicago Strike of June–July 1894.* Washington, D.C.: Government Printing Office, 1895.

Vale, Lawrence T. *Purging the Poorest: Public Housing and the Design of Politics of Twice-Cleared Communities.* Chicago: University of Chicago Press, 2013.

Various editions of the *Chicago Daily News, Chicago Defender, Chicago Democrat* and *Chicago Tribune.*

Winling, LaDale. "The Hunt for Restrictive Covenants in Cook County." *Newberry Magazine,* Spring/Summer 2022.

INDEX

K

King, Martin Luther, Jr. 17, 88, 96, 102

P

Parsons, Albert 49, 52, 58
Parsons, Lucy 21, 48
Prohibitory Liquor Laws 38
Pullman, George 60, 64, 68

S

Sandburg, Carl 80, 84
Socialistic Labor Party 49, 72

T

Thompson, William Hale "Big Bill" 79

W

Wells-Barnett, Ida B. 21, 71
Wentworth, John 25
Williams, Eugene 85, 87

ABOUT THE AUTHOR

J oseph Anthony Rulli is a transplanted Hoosier, living in Chicago since the fall of 2006. He has taught social studies, religion, philosophy and history at the high school level in Indiana. He began writing as a career on his arrival to his second city and has had three short stories published: "The Meating" (*New Stone Circle*, 2009), "Delayed" (*Echo Ink Review*, 2009) and "With This Ring" (*Over the Edge: The Edgy Writers Anthology*, 2017) and a stage play, *Let Me Just Say This*, performed in 2016. His books include *The Chicago Haymarket Affair: A Guide to a Labor Rights Milestone* (The History Press, 2016) and *Chicago Socialism: The People's History* (The History Press, 2019) as well as a satirical novel, *Bread & Circuses* (Shy City House, 2021). He has written a regular column and cultural reviews for the *Chicago Grid* and *Picture This Post*.

Visit us at
www.historypress.com